Team Performance on Fire!

4 Pillars to Skyrocket Team Productivity and
Boost Your Net-worth, Self-worth, and Joy-worth

John A. Williams, MSc

Published by Wellness Ink

Team Performance on Fire!

Proven Leadership Formula to Skyrocket Team Performance and Boost Your Networth, Self-worth, and Joy-worth.
By John A. Williams, MSc

Email: johnjaw47@gmail.com
Website: www.jawconsultancy.com
ISBN: 978-1-988645-31-5 (print)
ISBN: 978-1-988645-32-2 (digital)

Disclaimer

This book is for informational and educational purposes only. The author reserves the right to make any changes necessary to maintain the integrity of the information held within. This book is not intended to give legal, medical, and/or financial advice.

In no event shall the author or the publisher be responsible or liable for any loss of profits or other commercial or personal damages, including but not limited to special incidental, consequential, or any other damages, in connection with or arising out of furnishing, performance or use of this book.

Reading this book does not create a coach-client relationship between you and its author. This book is not a substitute for dedicated guidance.

Published by Wellness Ink
Interior Design by Polgarus Studio
Printed in the USA

Gifts and Bonuses for You

Team Performance on Fire! is based on a people-centered approach to leadership with a primary focus on business and project managers.

As my cordial thank-you for obtaining this book, please enjoy these three gifts and two bonuses that will help you further on your leadership journey.

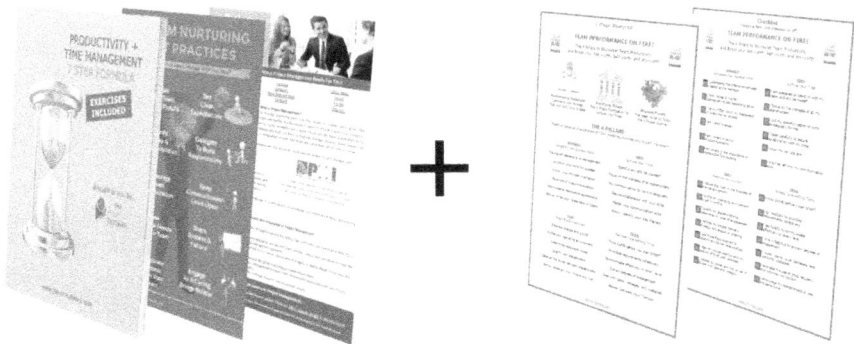

Free Guide: Productivity + Time Management 7 Step Formula
Everyone has unique needs when it comes to maximizing efficiency for optimal productivity. If your goal is to accomplish more in less time, then the 7 Step Formula is what you need. Make the seven described steps the foundation of your workweek.

Free Infographic: 10 Team Nurturing Best Practices
A visual reminder of how to lead from your heart and manage with your head. The content fits seamlessly with the intention of this book.

Free Cheat Sheet: Project Management Cheat Sheet
A time-saver which allows you to more effectively research project management. Contains links that take you to a vast variety of knowledge and information about the exciting world of project management, including ideas to monetize your knowledge of project management.

Bonuses: Blueprint and Checklist
In this package you will also receive a 1-Page Blueprint and an interactive Checklist to help you keep track while you take in the learnings of this book.

To get this package of gifts and bonuses, just go to:
https://www.jawconsultancy.com/team-performance-gifts

Enjoy!

John

Praise for the Author

Top professional in Pragmatic Leadership

In 2016 the author was recognized as a top professional in Pragmatic Leadership. For that occasion his signature pragmatic approach to leadership, the foundation for this book, was quoted on mainstream news outlets.

Quote:

'Mastering the human factor in leadership is the way to go to get the right things done and skyrocket your productivity. That's what successful high performing leaders do. It's all about how you connect and communicate, how you coax and coach, how you secure collaboration and commitment.'

As Seen On: ⓒCBS NEWS **FOX** 🅝NBC 🆎

Tremendous value on how to improve leadership posture

John A. Williams has captured a very pragmatic perspective on leadership with his light, very readable, book—*Team Performance on Fire!* Rich in case study stories, the book takes the reader on a step by step process for building a hopeful and optimistic vision for the future. John creates an environment where the reader can start at the beginning, middle (or even the end), and find tremendous value on how to improve their leadership posture.

~ *Carl Pritchard, PMP, PMI-RMP, Author of* **Risk Management: Concepts & Guidance, 5th Ed.**

Pragmatic leadership formula could be applied to any endeavor

Pragmatic, easy to read and to the point. The pragmatic leadership formula could be applied to any endeavor, including to teams fostering and developing modern quantitative enterprise risk management programs.

~ Dr F. Oboni, PhD, CEO of Riskope

Guide to reducing project risk and increasing project success

This book is for project managers who recognize that they need to make the shift from manager to leader, which is not only critically important for anyone working with a team of millennials but also one which hugely increases the bandwidth and skill set available to the leader, reducing project risk and increasing project success.

Leaders lead individuals, motivating, inspiring and enabling them to achieve more than they ever thought they could. Managers manage tasks, job roles and performance data, focusing time and energy on managing out the human factors that introduce uncertainty into their management plans. However, experience shows us that while you can omit the human factor in your management practice, you can't omit the human factor in your management results.

Humans like community, individual recognition, reward and fun. They hate to feel managed but like to follow leaders they trust and who they believe will help them to succeed. John's book provides a clear and pragmatic guide to how you too can be such a leader and reap the rewards of successful projects for yourself, your teams and your employers.

Accessible, fast-paced and comprehensive, this book will be referred to time and time again to refresh understanding and help identify new tools to lead effectively in new situations.

~ Dade Brown, Senior Business Transformation Manager, Senior PM, CEO of Enthous Ltd

Dedication

This book is dedicated to all the business and project leaders who can use some help and guidance in bringing out the best in their tribe.

Contents

Foreword
by Douglas M. Brown, PhD, PgMP

In 30 years of participating in, leading and observing projects, the one constant factor has been that success or failure is not determined by the difficulty of the project content. It is determined by the behavior of the project participants. The behavior in turn depends on the project manager's ability to work with the non-scientific, non-quantitative aspects of the project. An effective manager has to master the skills and processes of getting people to do things: in other words, politics at the organizational and team level. The problem is where one can learn how to do that. John A. Williams has at last given us the answer with *Team Performance on Fire!*

Many management courses include most of the tools in *Team Performance on Fire!*, but their contrived "case studies" make the tools appear to be unrealistic theories, and they are forgotten as soon as the course exam is passed. In contrast, John's four-pillar method shows you an orchestrated approach that focuses on getting the job done. His clear explanations of how he has applied these tools and skills in real-world situations allow you to revisit familiar but seldom-used tools such as the Force Field Analysis and understand them in a vibrant, cohesive leadership approach.

I'd offer one caveat for the average project manager. The main point of John's book is that a successful project depends on a project leader, not a project administrator. If you don't really have the empathy to care much about building up the people on the team, if you'd rather just work the tools, then this book's not really for you. Nor, frankly, is project leadership.

For professional project managers desiring to lead their teams to success, John has provided a superb one-stop guide to coping with the human dimensions of a project. It's not an "MBA in a box;" it's all the things that should have been (but weren't) taught in the MBA course in a box. Make sure it's in your toolkit.

Douglas M. Brown, PhD
Founder, Decision Integration LLC
Best-Selling Author of *Let It Simmer: How to Make Program, Portfolio and Project Management Practices Stick in a Skeptical Organization*

Alexandria, Virginia, USA
February 2019

How to Get the Best Experience with This Interactive Book

It's my honor and pleasure to bring you this interactive book. I recognize that as a business or project manager, you don't have the time nor the need to read hundreds of pages and cut your way through the fluff to get to the meat. So I kept this book short and succinct.

I like to overdeliver, yet not overwhelm you. I structured this book in a manner similar to how you would serve a meal, building in informational layers for your convenience. Let me explain what I mean by serving it up to you as a tasteful menu.

Appetizer

Overview of the core content to whet your appetite for the main course.

Main course

The in-depth core chapters.

Side dishes

Bonus chapters which are not mandatory but fortify the experience.

Flavor

Real-life case studies which illustrate a typical use of the content.

Delights

Infographics and other illustrations as visual reminders.

Takeaways

Calls-for-Action and Calls-for-Reflection to consolidate the content.

I call this an interactive book because I have included links to videos, which I encourage you to watch when they are presented. Don't put it off until later. Later has a habit of never coming! They also make the most sense at the moment they appear.

The same applies to the Calls-for-Action and the Calls-for-Reflection. Address them as soon as they appear to benefit most from the book's content. After reading the entire book, you will be equipped to draft an action plan to work on your most pressing team performance issues.

At the end of the book, I also included an assessment resource chapter with a list of complimentary self-assessments to help you evaluate the state of your knowledge and experience in a variety of relevant skills and competencies.

And finally, you will get the best experience by following the book in the order it is written. The content is purposefully laid out in a particular sequence, which I explain in the Overview chapter.

Now that you know how to get the most out of this book, keep on reading! Don't postpone until sometime later. At least read the Introduction and Overview chapters for now and whet your appetite for the main course. Don't be surprised if you find yourself consuming the entire menu in one sitting.

I wish you enjoyable and beneficial reading!

Introduction

Are you a business or project manager and worried about your project going sour? Are you chasing your team to meet deadlines and budget requirements? Wouldn't you rather spend your time enjoying the results and profits of your endeavor?

Let me set the scene and walk you through the experience from an awful nightmare to a liberating relief, and in the process get you ready to be a Performance Rocketeer.

1. Awful nightmare

Time and again your team fails to meet your promised deadline and budget. You have all your management tools in place, but your project just slips through your fingers. At the end of the day, every stakeholder—your sponsor, your team, and you yourself—is frustrated and disappointed. And you take that feeling back home to your family. This is a surefire recipe for sleepless nights and awful nightmares.

2. Disastrous consequences

As it is, you and your business are suffering a loss of revenue and reputation. If you don't fix this performance issue soon, you can forget that overdue promotion, lose valuable clients or profitable projects, and in the worst case lose your business and livelihood. That isn't what you had in mind, right?

Well, you're not alone. I've been there too, and so have many others. And sadly enough, many more will probably follow. But not you, not anymore, because now you have the benefit of this book with an approach to bring you success.

3. Best practice solution

Many years ago I had enough of poor business results, and I decided to do something about it. So here's what I did.

- Gathered my decades of extensive best practice successes and failures.
- Surveyed dozens of seasoned business/program/project managers all operating under challenging conditions.
- Analyzed hundreds of successful and failed projects and business cases.
- Concluded that the human factor is the key to success.
- Designed, tested and tweaked a people-centered approach to leading teams successfully.
- Developed my proven signature Pragmatic Leadership Formula™.

Altogether, you're getting decades of knowledge and experience condensed in an easy-to-follow concept. The bottom line is that it's all about people, the most valuable asset in your project or business endeavor. By applying my formula you can nurture your team to skyrocket their performance, and in turn boost your net-worth, self-worth, and joy-worth.

You will discover how to:

- Excel as a people-centered leader rather than a spreadsheet manager.
- Jumpstart your mindset into success mode for change and growth.
- Secure collaboration with your team.
- Blend in with your team and still be yourself.

- Thrive by nurturing your tribe.
- Read the project environment to get in control.
- Harness the right tools to enforce your leadership with ease.

4. Liberating relief

This book elaborates on my signature formula, based on best practice, which has successfully been applied by myself and many others for decades. It's designed to give peace of mind when dealing with challenging projects and business endeavors. It also addresses how to cope with reluctant stakeholders in general and team members in particular.

5. Performance Rocketeer

If you want to take your team performance to the next level, then this book will help you do just that. The premise is that you are willing to do so in a people-centered manner. This book elaborates on the bar-none pragmatic people-centered approach to lead your tribe to unmatched, lasting high achievements.

Having the power of a super-motivated, proficient, and productive team at your disposal, will gain you the reputation of a credible and reliable goal getter! You will be a delight to your stakeholders and well-respected by your peers. You will be the Performance Rocketeer!

But what's in that for you? Well, being a Performance Rocketeer means that you're known for excelling the performance of your stakeholders in general and your team in particular. That reputation will boost your market value (net-worth), and also give you peace of mind to do your job in full confidence (self-worth). You will experience much more pleasure and satisfaction (joy-worth) in your work, and you will take that feeling back home to your family and loved ones. A win for your business and livelihood, a win for you, and a win for your home base. No more awful nightmares and disastrous consequences!

*"Nurture your tribe
and your tribe will carry you
all the way."*

~ The Pragmaticioner

Overview

The objective of this book is to help you skyrocket team performance and in turn boost your net-worth, self-worth, and joy-worth. You will do that through a people-centered pragmatic approach to leadership. So let me set the scene for this approach and give you an overview of what you can expect from this book. The quote is an opening teaser for the following sections of this chapter.

Command with Mindset
Fuel with Grit, Grip, and Gear
Ready, Set, Go!

The Foundation

This book is about leadership, not about management, and based on my signature Pragmatic Leadership Formula™. The kind of leadership that fires up your tribe to reach new heights in performance.

To motivate others to perform, best practice has shifted in the course of time from "Bossy" (Do what I say!) through "Managerial" (Got to cover my back!) to "Leading" (What can I do for them!). That's the logical consequence of the ever-growing empowerment of the workforce, aka tribe. More accessible and affordable education and knowledge gathering made this achievable.

Leaders and their tribe are on the same side of the playing field now. They need each other, and they rely on each other to accomplish their mutual goals. So just giving orders and using managerial tools alone will not cut it any longer.

My experience of decades and my survey among peers show that the real success factors are the right mindset and addressing the relational, situational and rational aspects of leadership. In that order! I call it the pragmatic approach to successful leadership with a wink. In short, a leader with the 3G mindset for change and growth.

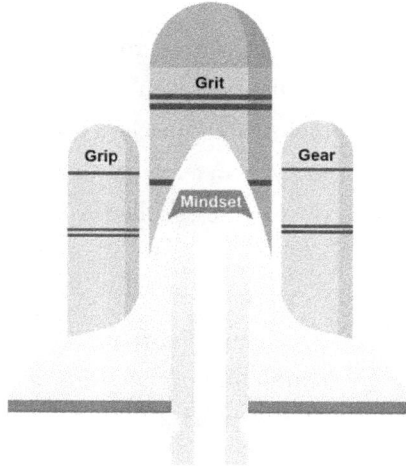

The three Gs stand for Grit, Grip, and Gear, respectively representing the relational, situational, and rational aspects of leadership. Such a leader also has a certain core attitude, the 5 Ps. And finally, the collaboration of all stakeholders is secured by the 2 Cs. Don't worry, the 5 Ps and 2 Cs will be explained in the Pillar chapters.

We use a pragmatic approach, because we want to be realistic and use our common sense. With a wink, because we want to express that we enjoy what we do and hopefully inspire our environment to embrace that feeling.

Now imagine yourself as the commander of that spaceship in the graphic, all fueled up and ready for takeoff. Taking your team under your wings to the heights of performance where you've never been before. Wouldn't that give you the feeling of being the Performance Rocketeer? Of course it will! That's why you're here.

In the back of this book you will find a full-page infographic showing how all the components mentioned above are boiled down into one simple formula.

The Pillar Concept

Now a formula can be very appealing, but how do we apply that in daily practice? Here is where this book comes into play. I address all the elements of the formula in four pillars. I adopt the term "pillar" from the Greek Parthenon building to symbolize the fortifying structure to help you as a leader to support and nurture your tribe. Each pillar has its own merits, but together they reinforce each other.

The puzzle graphic is another symbolic illustration of how the four pillars fit together to strengthen each other. It also shows the route by which to follow them. Altogether, this infographic is an example of a whole that is stronger than the mere sum of the individual parts. I call it the Routing Puzzle.

The graphic illustrates the level of importance of the pillars relative to each other. The Mindset Pillar is positioned at the top followed by Grit, Grip, and Gear in order of importance. Meaning, you need to be in the right mindset to successfully apply the teachings of the practical Grit and Grip Pillars. The Gear Pillar is of a more supportive nature.

Be the next Performance Rocketeer by applying the four fortifying pillars in the order given by the Routing Puzzle.

A note on my inspiring influencers

Just like any other successful leader, I also have my influencers, motivators, mentors, and coaches to inspire me and keep me on track. With respect to this book, I picked three prominent contemporary leadership and success advocates of superb quality whom I consider to be my guides. Every time I find myself in a leadership predicament, I try to imagine how these professionals would tackle my issue.

I'm referring to Bob Proctor (Proctor Gallagher Institute), John C. Maxwell (John Maxwell Team), and Kevin Kruse (LEADx). One way or another, they each embrace the human factor as a crucial element to success. And of course they are outstanding leaders themselves. From time to time I'll be quoting them throughout this book.

Here's why I picked these three visionaries with respect to this book.

Bob Proctor's paradigm shift approach is what I reflect on when I'm contemplating mindset. Proctor advocates changing habits in the subconscious mind through repetition of information to bring about a paradigm shift. The Mindset Pillar has much to do with paradigm shift.

John C. Maxwell's learnings on leadership keep me focused on nurturing people and their interests. His vast worldwide following of committed leaders in all kinds of endeavors is the living proof of the binding qualities he incorporates in his approach to leadership. The Grit and Grip Pillars thrive on a binding approach.

Kevin Kruse's insights on management and leadership keep me up to date with the prevailing best practices through his LEADx platform. He has a flawless antenna to pick up the latest practices in management. The Grit, Grip, and Gear Pillars correlate well with best practices.

I'm telling you about my mentors to encourage you to find your role models and influencers. Those who inspire you to be the best when you need it most. Try to attach a specific inspiration to each of them. That will help you focus on the motivational help that best suits your need in a particular situation, giving you that little mental push to move you forward.

Bird's-eye view

Now it's time for me to introduce each of the pillars from a bird's-eye view. I will use infographics to explain the four pillars in this overview. Consider them your pillar reference and anchor. In the chapters that follow I will go into depth about each pillar. This way I ease you slowly but surely into the main course. And to top it all off, I will end this overview with an acronymic twist on the four pillars.

Pillar #1: Mindset

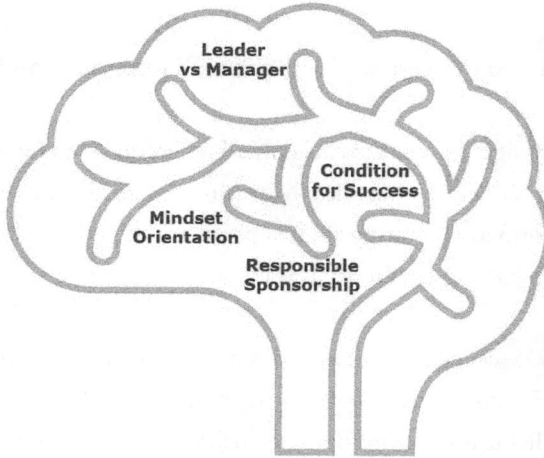

The Mindset Pillar begins with my take on the difference between a leader and a manager to get you in the leadership state of mind. Then I will show you how to condition your mind for success, followed by finding your mindset orientation. After that, I will address some specific areas to further fortify your mindset for success.

The goal here is to jumpstart your mindset into success mode for change and growth. This pillar will provide you the best preparation to follow up with the remaining pillars. The graphic above illustrates the components to help you envision your golden key to magnificence in leadership.

Pillar #2: Grit

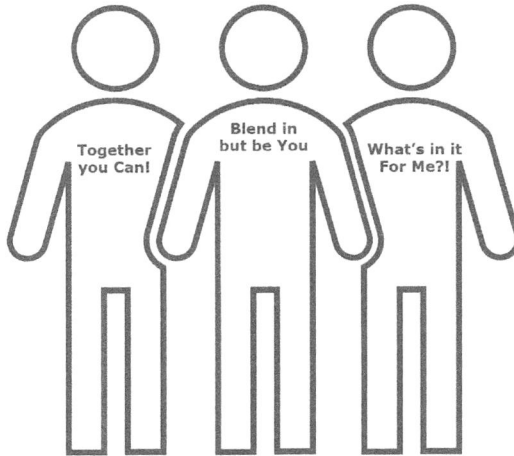

In this pillar, I focus on creating relationships based on respect and understanding of the interests of each stakeholder. These relationships are the foundation for your success as a leader.

Know that you are dealing with human beings, people in various roles with a variety of personal and professional interests. By building a relationship you gain and give confidence and trust. You need to ensure an environment which grants you success in achieving your ultimate goal; otherwise, you stand alone in your endeavor. It's all about being the leader with grit. You draw the line, but you secure the collaboration of your stakeholders.

Pillar #3: Grip

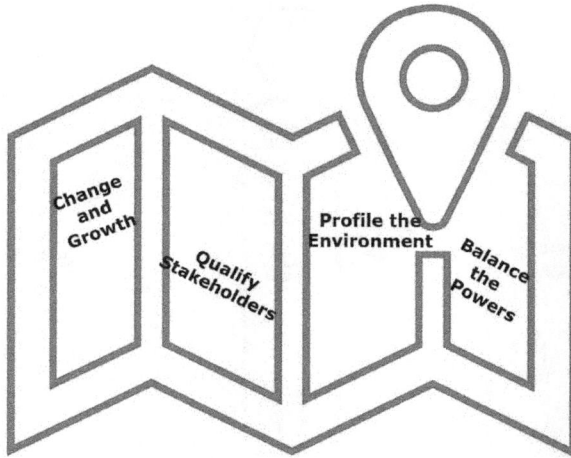

In this pillar, I discuss environmental circumstances of a project, and tailoring the leader's approach to deal with these circumstances. Getting the right stakeholders to do the right things in the right order to achieve the desired results. Reading and profiling the environment and securing control. Applying power and influence.

In principle, each project result aims to bring about change and growth in the organization. A fitting adage for this goal would be "Improving, Changing, Anchoring."

Pillar #4: Gear

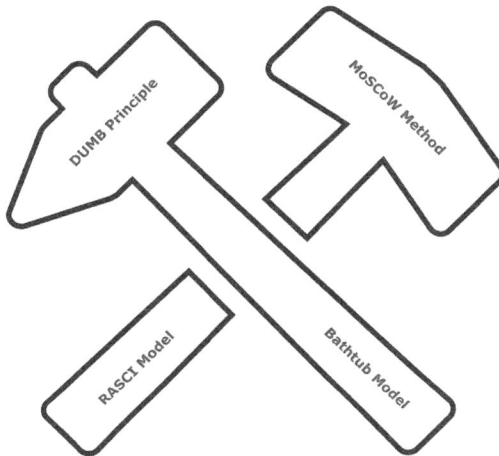

This pillar deals with some useful leadership tools. There are many management methods and approaches out there. This book is about leadership, not management. Of course, there are some traditional management tools that a leader will use, but those don't fall within the scope of this book.

I will suggest a few basic tools that I believe are very useful for a pragmatic leader to set the right conditions. They will help you secure the collaboration of all your stakeholders.

Acronymic Twist

Let me end this overview with a playful twist: a striking acronymic interpretation of the four pillars.

M.I.N.D.S.E.T.
Mentally Internalize Noble Directive Statement Envisioning Triumph

G.R.I.T.
Grow Relational Interactive Teams

G.R.I.P.
Gain Robust Information Position

G.E.A.R.
Give Everyone Accountable Responsibilities

Now that you've got a sneak peek of the four pillars, go ahead and dive into the more profound learnings behind each one of them. And most of all, take action on the four pillars to fire up your tribe to new heights in performance. Start with the Mindset Pillar to set you up for success.

Pillar #1: Mindset

"Envision your golden key to magnificence."

The Mindset Pillar is the most vital pillar of them all. The chapters falling under this pillar will set you up for success and prepare you to get the most profit out of the pillars that follow. Take a good look at the graphic above. It illustrates your envisioned golden key to magnificence in leadership that you offer to the world. Let's make it happen!

Chapter 1.0: Jumpstart your mindset into success mode for change and growth

In my opinion, the state of your mind determines whether you are successful or not. I learned that the hard way in my own practice, and many of my successful peers confirmed they went through the same experience. One may even argue that this truth applies to any aspect of life.

Your mindset comes through in your body language and transfers that state to your tribe. That first impression of you standing tall in your belief in your endeavor is crucial. It gives you an edge when you address your team about your vision and goals.

Let's face it, if you don't show up emitting confidence and belief in what you stand for, why should others follow your lead? Your stakeholders and team members have that built-in antenna to sense you out. That's their basic instinct at work.

Successful application of the following pillars in this book will be very difficult without the right mindset which in this case should be a mindset for success. That's why I claim the Mindset Pillar to be the most important of the four. In this pillar I will discuss various subjects that will help you get in the mindset for success and prepare you mentally for your pragmatic leadership.

At first glance, you may think that some subjects seem farfetched or even weird, but once you see them in perspective, you will grasp their meaning and power. So, bear with me and go through the process. After all, mindset is not a tangible attribute.

Mindset is something you have to open up to and experience. By training your conscious mind to achieve the things you want, you will gradually condition your subconscious mind to make it a habit. This pillar will help you get in success mode and in the habit of achieving success.

"Thoughts become things. If you see it in your mind, you will hold it in your hand." ~ Bob Proctor

Remember that the goal here is to jumpstart your mindset in success mode before you dive into the following pillars to set your team performance on fire, and in turn boost your net-worth, self-worth, and joy-worth.

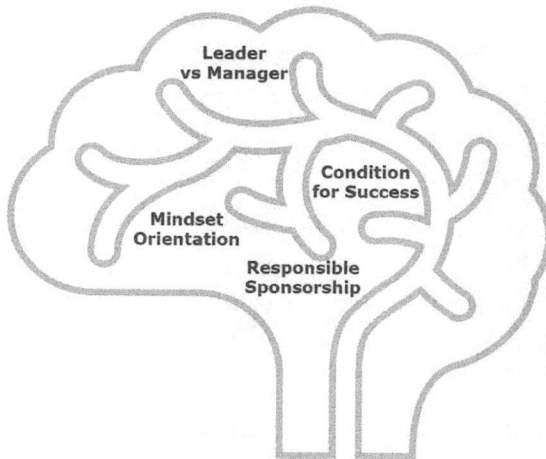

As stated earlier, I will begin by contrasting leaders and managers, then show you techniques to create and strengthen your success mindset.

In the Case Study chapter, I share with you my personal first major success story that changed my life completely. All just based on mindpower and knowing my why! It's proof that a success mindset does make a difference. If

I can achieve that at such an early stage in life, I'm confident you can achieve anything with all that life experience you have under your belt. All you need is the right mindset. The mindset for success.

In the next chapter, I will give you my take on the difference between managers and leaders.

Chapter 1.1: A people-centered leader or a spreadsheet manager

Many leaders in business, communities or projects are not as lastingly successful as they could be. Why? Because they rely on the more rational aspects of leadership such as methods, techniques, and tools. They manage rather than take the lead. Their perceived leadership is mostly defined by facts and figures in a spreadsheet and managing the process, not by leading their tribe—the human factor—which in my experience is paramount to success and satisfaction.

"Management is doing things right; leadership is doing the right things."
~ Peter F. Drucker

"Managers work with processes; leaders work with people."
~ John C. Maxwell

Many prominent leaders have given their similar take on this matter in their own words. Here is my succinct and bold interpretation in a few sound bites and a catchy illustration.

Managers manage things, do things right, and cover their backs.

Leaders lead people, do the right things, and nurture their tribe.

Managers are driven by rationale. Leaders are driven by passion.

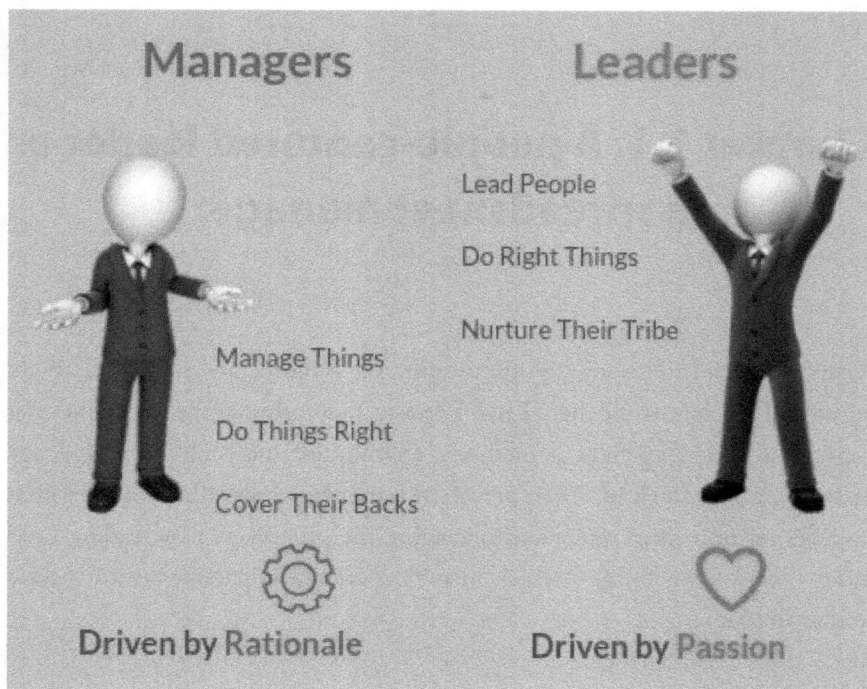

Managers

Manage Things

Do Things Right

Cover Their Backs

Driven by Rationale

Leaders

Lead People

Do Right Things

Nurture Their Tribe

Driven by Passion

"A great leader's courage to fulfill his vision comes from passion, not position." ~
John C. Maxwell

Mastering the human factor in leadership is a prerequisite to get the right things done and skyrocket team performance. That's what successful high-performing leaders do. It's all about how you connect and communicate, coax and coach, secure collaboration and commitment. Whether you take the lead in business, community, or family affairs, at the end of the day, it's the people involved and their environment that matter. They define your level of success or failure!

Of course, a leader will also use management tools in the sense I mentioned before. Even people-centered leaders will have to deal with processes and employ facts and figures to run their business or project. My point is that leaders put their tribe first and foremost and then manage things in the background. To emphasize my point, I call them people-centered pragmatic leaders. Managers tend to do it the other way around.

Understanding the difference between leaders and managers as I've explained it is crucial. My signature approach in this book is focused on the concept of people-centered pragmatic leadership.

Now it's up to you. Wouldn't you rather be a pragmatic people-centered leader than just a spreadsheet manager?

To get in the flow, listen to what Roselinde Torres has to say in her TED Talk on what it takes to be a great leader. https://bit.ly/1q6Sssd

In the next chapter, I will explore leadership skills that distinguish great leaders in different fields.

Chapter 1.2: Distinguishing skills from great leaders

Addressing leadership would not be complete if I didn't elaborate on leadership skills. There are library shelves full of books on leadership traits through the centuries—leadership skills based on a variety of whether-or-not scientific approaches. As a pragmatic leader, I take another angle of approach.

Through careful analysis and research, I came up with ten leadership skills that repeatedly show up when looking at great leaders in different fields. To be honest, I wasn't a bit surprised that these skills turn out to be all people-oriented. They not only fit seamlessly into my approach to leadership, but they also confirm my approach from the practice of great leaders.

I'm not presenting an exhaustive list of traits every leader has. What I'm offering is a list of leadership qualities that every one of us should adopt into our daily lives. Even if you don't want to lead, you can still use these powerful skills to help you succeed in anything you want.

These are the ten key leadership skills I believe everyone should possess:

1. Vision
2. Passion
3. Confidence
4. Positive Attitude
5. Persistence
6. Communication
7. Creativity/Innovation
8. Independence
9. Integrity
10. Ability to Delegate

Now let's examine each skill a bit closer and illustrate each with an example of a leader who prominently excels in that skill.

1. Vision

The concept of "vision" is all about having a vivid mental image of what you want to accomplish. The vision in your mind should be so clear and strong that it will help make your goal become a reality.

Responsible entrepreneurs, sponsors, business leaders, and project leaders will start their endeavor by carefully crafting a vision statement. These statements will communicate the overall goals of their business.

A good vision statement will include three elements:

*   Your Purpose
*   Your Goals
*   Your Values

A great leader needs to start with a powerful vision for his goal. It is so much easier to lead people when you have a concrete idea of where you want to go.

Research shows that when employees or team members find a vision statement meaningful, they are 18 percent more likely to be engaged than average. Your vision will keep you on track.

The best leaders have a vision that follows the three elements above, and they will not waver from its path until they reach their goal.

> *"Vision without action is just a dream, action without vision just passes the time, and vision with action can change the world." ~ Nelson Mandela*
>
> Nelson Mandela had a vision of the end of apartheid. He fought endlessly for this vision and even spent many years in jail because of it. But he never wavered. His vision and conviction were so compelling that eventually, he succeeded. He lived not only to see the end of apartheid but to become the first president of South Africa.

2. Passion

Passion intrinsically links to vision. A good vision should certainly match with your passion.

The word "passion" gets tossed around quite a bit. It is almost a buzzword. That doesn't make it any less important, though.

We just need to realize that passion isn't simply some flippant idea that is fun to chat about and discuss. It's real, and it's necessary. It also isn't only about enjoying something. It is about needing something.

If you have a passion, you wake up and fall asleep thinking about it. When you are doing something else, you will catch yourself thinking about your dream.

Leaders need to have passion because that's what makes them tick. Imagine you are a leader and you're working on two projects. One is a passion project that you are completely beholden to. The other is some simple busywork that you have to do to make ends meet. Which one is going to motivate you?

More importantly, which one is going to help you motivate the people you lead? People aren't stupid, and we know when our leaders are faking it. If you feel passionate about something, then it will emanate from every pore of your being.

Great leaders feel **passionate** about their **vision**. It's this **passion** that allows them to make sure their **vision** becomes a **reality**.

"We ourselves feel that what we are doing is just a drop in the ocean. But if that drop were not there, I think the ocean would be less by that missing drop." ~ Mother Theresa

While she was a quiet and tiny woman, Mother Theresa made up for her small size with an unbelievable reservoir of passion. She wasn't working for glory or fame. She was doing what she believed she was put on this earth to accomplish. She spent 50 years working among the poorest people in the world. The missionary order she founded is now active in 133 countries, still doing the work she was so passionate about to this day.

---

3. Confidence

Having confidence is one of the most successful leadership skills there is.

Confidence is simply the belief that you can rely on someone or something.

When put in those words, it is obvious why confidence is such an important leadership trait. If you are a leader, then you need to believe in a LOT of different things:

- Your vision
- Yourself
- Your team
- Your ideas
- Your plans
- Your decisions
- Etc.

Good leaders don't just have confidence. They exude it. They don't just act confidently, but they inspire others to as well. Having a vision is great and being passionate about it helps as well. However, if you aren't confident in yourself or your team's ability to pull it off—you have nothing.

People can spot a lack of confidence a mile away. If you want to build genuine connections in your life—be it personal or business—then you need to be confident.

> *"I feel confident because I'm the best player in the world. It's simple."* ~ *LeBron James*
>
> LeBron James came into a man's sport, while still a kid. He hit the league as an 18-year-old phenom, with the weight of expectation like no athlete ever before, and he instantly dominated.
>
> He gave the above quote a few years ago when he was locked in a Finals battle with one of the greatest teams ever assembled in the NBA. His team (The Cavs) were down in the series and huge underdogs—but his confidence didn't waver. In a legacy-defining moment, LeBron and the Cavs ended up defeating the odds and winning the championship that year.

4. Positive Attitude

A positive attitude may seem a lot like confidence, but they are two different things.

A positive attitude means that you look at things in a positive light. You don't dwell on negativity, you see the good in bad situations, and you feel happy. You make a conscious effort to find and see the benefit in every situation.

Leaders need to have a positive attitude because it will help them deal with their journey. The road is never smooth, so staying positive is key. It also helps to build the morale and motivation of your team. If you show up ready to tackle the world, your team will too. A positive attitude is contagious!

Life is not all gumdrops and lollipops, but we all have a choice to make. We can choose to dwell on the negative and get swallowed up by it, or we can choose to stay positive and battle through the dark times.

You don't have to be positive all the time. You will have moments of grief and sadness in your life. Take the time you need to wallow. But always keep in mind that there are good things and good people out there, and you deserve them.

"The more you praise and celebrate your life, the more there is in life to celebrate." ~ Oprah Winfrey

Oprah walks it as she talks it. She not only possesses a positive attitude; her entire brand is based around helping other people achieve the same.

This self-made mogul has countless articles and quotes in which she shares the importance of positive thinking. She doesn't just talk about positive thinking; she is a glowing example of just how powerful it can be.

5. Persistence

Persistence is the ability to continue toward your goals in spite of difficulty or obstacles. Almost all success has come after someone has persisted through some difficulty. We hear the term "overnight success" mentioned a lot, but most often there is an example of persistence buried beneath it.

Leaders need to persist because they never reach a goal without some obstacle or hardship.

Leaders need to be ready to face obstacles head-on, and if their team gets knocked down, then it is up to them to get the team back up to take another run at it.

The ability to persist is often the single trait that turns failure into success.

"Profound belief in something allows every individual to find an immense inner force, and to overcome his or her failings." ~ Soichiro Honda

The first name might not be familiar to you, but the last name certainly is. Soichiro Honda is a stunning example of the power of persistence.

During World War II, he owned a company that produced parts for Toyota—it was bombed and destroyed. Instead of giving up, he sold the salvageable parts of his company to Toyota and started a new company. It was a little company you may have heard of: Honda Motor Company.

6. Communication

The ability to communicate allows you to share your vision, or ideas with the rest of the world. Most often this will be accomplished either verbally or in writing.

A lot goes into being a capable communicator, but if you can effectively convey your messages, then you have the basics covered.

This is vitally important for a leader, because who would follow someone who can't properly explain:

- What they believe in
- What their goals are
- What they expect from you

Leaders might not be dynamic public speakers, but they need to be able to convey their ideas. They could have the best ideas in the room (or world!) but if they can't explain them, who cares?

Everyday leaders are dealing with other people and trying to get across some point. They need to be able to express their feelings to others. More importantly, they need to be able to do it in a way that doesn't offend and allows them to get what they want more easily.

I don't mean lying or manipulation! Leaders simply need to be able to convey their sometimes-complex thoughts in an easy to understand manner.

"People fail to get along because they fear each other; they fear each other because they don't know each other; they don't know each other because they have not communicated with each other." ~ Martin Luther King, Jr.

Martin Luther King, Jr., was one of the leading voices in the civil rights movement. I use the term "voice" quite literally.

His ability as an orator is legendary. While his contributions to society are wide and vast, almost every single one of us knows about "I Have a Dream…".

You can debate how important this one speech was in the overall scheme of things, but you can't argue that we'll always remember it.

7. Creativity/Innovation

Creativity is using your imagination to come up with original and unique ideas.

Innovation isn't the same thing, but they are very closely linked. Innovation is the action of creating new methods, ideas, or things.

So while they aren't exactly the same, it would be pretty hard to have innovation without creativity.

Great leaders need to be creative because one of their key responsibilities will be problem-solving. Sometimes to solve a difficult problem, you are going to have to think creatively. You might need to come up with a solution that no one has ever come up with before—and THAT is innovation!

Sometimes the solution is quite apparent and straightforward, but sometimes we need to think outside of the box. Other times, the "apparent solution" isn't the best one.

Sometimes a little creativity will allow us to come up with a solution that is even *better* than the straightforward one.

> *"The path to the CEO's office should not be through the CFO's office, and it should not be through the marketing department. It needs to be through engineering and design." -* Elon Musk
>
> Elon Musk likes to zig when everyone else zags. That is just who he is as a person. One thing that is so impressive about his ability to innovate is his full commitment to it. He wasn't afraid to take on big auto and create his electric car. He wasn't happy just sticking to that either. He went on to create household battery systems, started work on something called a "hyperloop," oh and he is also dabbling in driverless cars and casual space exploration for the masses. Like the man or not, you can't say he doesn't commit to big, audacious, innovative ideas.

8. Independence

Independence has a few different meanings, but what we are talking about here is the ability to do what you want without worrying about what other people think.

Independent leaders will take chances that people don't always find agreeable. They will make unpopular choices. They won't be afraid to march to the beat of their own drum. If they genuinely believe in something, they will do everything they can to make it happen.

Independence is an important leadership trait, because sometimes taking that unpopular risk is what is going to take your team to the next level.

A lot of people are comfortable just flying under the radar and doing only the things asked of them. Great leaders aren't afraid to step on toes to make something happen.

You need to be able to figure out what it is you want, and then make independent decisions on how to get there. Don't let doubters or societal norms (aka what we're expected to do) hold you back.

"In order to be irreplaceable one must always be different." ~ Coco Chanel

Coco Chanel was never scared to do or say what she wanted. In a time when women were supposed to act and look a certain way, she wasn't having any of it.

She helped liberate women from the classic corset by popularizing a much more casual standard of style. She became a fashion icon because she did and said what she wanted, even if it wasn't in vogue at the time.

---

9. Integrity

A lot of times people will use the terms integrity and honesty interchangeably.

While it is true that honesty is a big part of integrity, it isn't the entirety of it. Integrity also means that you have strong principles, values, and expectations.

More importantly, your actions are consistent with those terms.

For a leader, integrity is vitally important. Being honest is one of the best ways to build trust, and as a leader, you need people to trust you. Who wants an untrustworthy leader?

The second half of the definition is just as important. When you have values and principles that you consistently live up to, your team will begin to recognize it. People will value knowing where they stand with you, as well as where you yourself stand on issues of principle.

Having integrity means you are consistent, and being consistent makes people comfortable.

Having integrity also indicates that you have morals that guide your life. That means different things to different people, but there is power in having values that guide you. It helps you make tough decisions. It makes you more trustworthy. It ensures that you stay true to yourself.

"No man has a good enough memory to be a successful liar." ~ Abraham Lincoln

It might not be the most exciting handle, but Lincoln was known as Honest Abe for a reason. He was committed to honesty and his morals. He had strong beliefs about certain things and even went through a painful war to live up to them.

Not only did he act as an example of integrity, but he also wrote about its importance as well. You can find countless quotes from the man on the subject. Honest Abe, indeed.

---

10. Ability to Delegate

Delegation is the ability to assign, entrust and transfer certain responsibilities to other people. It's important not only to be able to assign people certain tasks but to trust in their ability to accomplish them.

That is important for leaders because it allows them three main benefits:

- They take things off their plate so they can focus their efforts toward more pressing tasks.
- If a leader lacks a certain skill set, he or she can offset that by letting someone more adept take over.
- Leaders empower other people by rewarding them with responsibility.

Delegation is a win-win-win!

Leaders can reduce their workload while increasing efficiency and team morale.

The delegation of tasks will free up your time. It will free up your energy. And most importantly, it allows you to address your weaknesses by bringing in more experienced or talented contributors.

"Delegate almost to the point of abdication." ~ Warren Buffet

Warren Buffet is probably the most successful investor of our time. He is one of the wealthiest people in the world with a net worth of around 90 billion dollars. To say he is successful might be an understatement.

Can you believe, then, that investors in his business worried about the man delegating too much? Buffet's management style can be summed up by his quote above. His theory is that by delegating, he is empowering the executives below him. Question the man all you want, but you can't argue with his results!

In the next chapter, I will show you how to condition your mind for success to achieve your purpose.

Chapter 1.3: How to condition your mind for success

When you start a new project, of course you want that project to succeed, even if you know it will be a great challenge. That is especially true with big projects regarding duration and budget. So, if you want to succeed then let's condition your mind for success. Let's get you in the success mode. There is a saying that nothing succeeds like success.

Without diving into the deeper workings of neuroscience, I will explore three mind-conditioning features.

1. The sense of sight, which refers to the influence of modeling.
2. The sense of hearing, which refers to the influence of verbal programming.
3. Specific incidents that play a part in determining our perception of success.

I will address the influence of modeling with visualization, and the influence of verbal programming with declaration. I know, it seems daunting, but hold on to your seat—it's not that hard. Here we go.

Write down in the present tense your Statement of Intent for your new project. Be specific and realistic about your WHAT, your WHEN and your HOW.

- WHAT will your project contribute? Your objective.
- WHEN do you deliver the results? Your delivery date.
- HOW will you realize your goals? Your actions.

Example: "I will increase sales profits by 10 percent by the end of December 2018 by reducing costs in the sales process."

Your WHAT	Your WHEN	Your HOW
I will increase sales profits by 10 percent	By the end of December 2018	By reducing costs in the sales process

Now hold your hands up and cup them together and envision a golden key resting in your hands. It's as if you are offering this golden key to the world to unlock the benefits of your project. This golden key symbolizes the success of your project, and you feel happy and proud to present it to the world. See that golden key shining in your cupped hands—use your imagination. You stand tall!

Read your Statement of Intent out loud in that posture with your imaginary golden key in your cupped hands. Repeat your declaration until it is naturally programmed in your mind. Put enthusiasm and positive energy into it. Declare it like you truly mean it NOW. Read it every day until it becomes second nature to you.

Also, write down your Statement of Intent on a large sheet of paper—big and bold—and hang it in your office and your home. Place it where you're bound to see it every day. Every day and every night, stand in front of it with your cupped hands visualizing the golden key and say your declaration out loud five times.

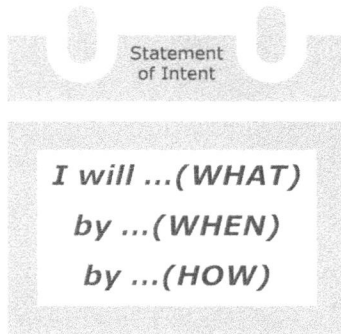

Statement
of Intent

I will ...(WHAT)
by ...(WHEN)
by ...(HOW)

Somewhere along the line, surely some incidents made you feel happy and proud. Maybe the birth of your child, a promotion, anything. Something that made you feel tall, no matter how big or small. Reproduce that feeling in your mind. It puts a big smile on your face. You feel successful and on top of the world. Hold on to that feeling, that emotion, and recall that feeling when you are saying your declaration out loud.

By all means cultivate positive thoughts like desire, faith, gratitude, hope, inspiration, joy, love, pride. They make your golden key shine even more. Don't underestimate the power of declaration and visualization. Just do it for a while and surprise yourself. Some psychologists say it takes 21 days to change a habit. So, why not do this for at least 21 days and fix your habit for success. Successful leaders step out of their comfort zone and explore new horizons. You have nothing to lose and all to gain!

The power of this mindset approach is that you not only internalize your purpose, your WHY. You also see, feel and experience the sweetness of this successful project as if it has already happened. It makes you confident and credible when you address your tribe about your goal. You radiate the success of the project to your tribe. Your tribe catches your positive vibes, now they also believe in the successful outcome, and they are ready to go for it. You've got your mindset in success mode, and also that of your tribe!

For some extra inspiration, check out Simon Sinek's TED Talk about focusing on your WHY (your purpose).
https://bit.ly/2IyBl20

The next chapter will take you on a parable journey to anchor your mindset orientation.

Chapter 1.4: Anchor your mindset orientation with the ancient parable of the Japanese stonecutter

Long ago Zen Master Joji traveled through the Kobe valley.

One day he saw a man working in a quarry. He approached the worker and asked him what he was doing. The man didn't look at him and just grunted: "Well, that's obvious, isn't it—I'm cutting stones." The traveler continued on his way.

After a few hours, he passed another quarry and also here he saw a man working, surrounded by a large pile of stones. Joji asked him about the nature of his work. The man looked up, smiled and said: "I am cutting stones in this quarry and with the yield, I feed myself and my family." The traveler thanked him and proceeded on his journey.

When the sun reached his summit, Joji looked for a place to rest, and he found a place in the shade in a third quarry. Also here he saw a man at work, surrounded by an even larger pile of stones, and Master Joji also asked him what he was doing. The man stood up, offered his guest a drink and said: "I take the stones from this quarry and remodel them to building stones. With the money I earn with this I feed myself, my family and my family-in-law who live with us too. But if you really want to know what I am doing, you have to travel for another two days. Because there they are building a splendid, holy temple with my stones."

This parable of the Japanese stonecutter is a metaphoric illustration of the basic three mindset orientations:

- **Task:** Cutting stones
- **Goal:** Cutting stones to feed the family
- **Vision:** Remodeling stones to build a holy temple

Successful leaders contribute to magnificence and legacy. Successful leaders are vision oriented! They think big and know how their contribution will affect, change and improve people and environments.

"Great leaders always seem to embody two seemingly disparate qualities. They are both highly visionary and highly practical." ~ John C. Maxwell

Anchor your mind on vision orientation. Remind yourself of the parable of the Japanese stonecutter, visualize that magnificent proverbial holy temple that will be your legacy, and you are good to go.

The next chapter is about the sleeping lion of miscommunication.

Chapter 1.5: Be aware of miscommunication

Whenever you have more people working together for a common cause, it becomes imperative that the right hand knows what the left hand is doing so that there is no miscommunication. There will be times that it happens, but those occasions need to be rare.

Leadership is working with people, so be aware of the human factor where communication and perception are essential. Look at the illustration and see how the different stakeholders may interpret the same expression. The different symbols in the circles of the stakeholders illustrate the difference in interpretation.

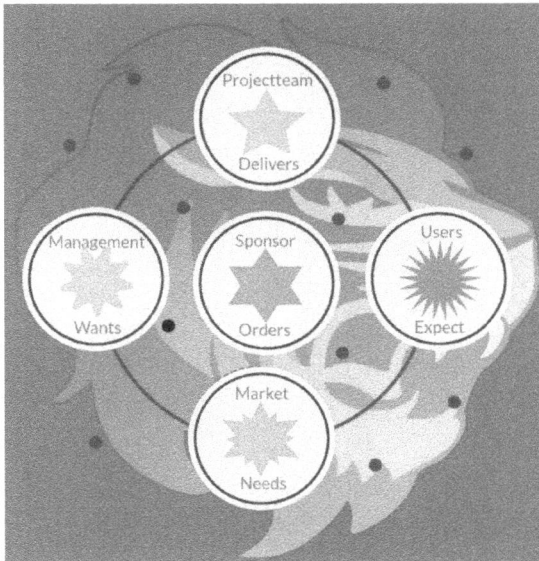

The single point I want to get across here is for you to be aware of the sleeping lion of miscommunication. Be vigilant, or it will devour you!

Check and re-check for conformity in understanding the message. Insist that the stakeholders explain in their own words how they interpret the message. Make sure that in the end, all stakeholders have the same interpretation. Of course, this should be the interpretation you want them to embrace.

In the next chapter, you will learn more about responsible sponsorship.

Chapter 1.6: The importance of responsible sponsorship

Sponsorship is an essential part of successful project delivery, whether you are a single empowered manager or a steering committee providing direction for the project.

Managerial decisions are a regular part of moving through the project life cycle and must be made efficiently to keep the project moving forward. The changes that result from the project's execution will have to be endorsed. Without appropriate sponsorship, this is very unlikely to happen, and the benefits of the project will not be realized.

One of the traits of a successful leader is to grasp the importance of responsible sponsorship. A responsible sponsor not only seeks business success, but also strives for added value to the community. A successful sponsor should ideally have the following personal skills:

- Persuasiveness
- Bringing together business interests and social significance
- Indicates purpose
- Awareness of the added value
- Motivated for the long-term
- Sense of responsibility
- Decisive
- Living and breathing the significance of responsible sponsorship

International studies have shown that many major projects fail because of poor sponsorship. As a leader, you often have to deal with sponsors yourself, for instance in the case of you leading a sponsored project. On the other hand, you are also a kind of sponsor to your team, your tribe. Maybe more than any other stakeholder, as a sponsor, you must be fully aware of your WHY, your purpose. That will give you the edge to be credible and trustworthy in getting your message across.

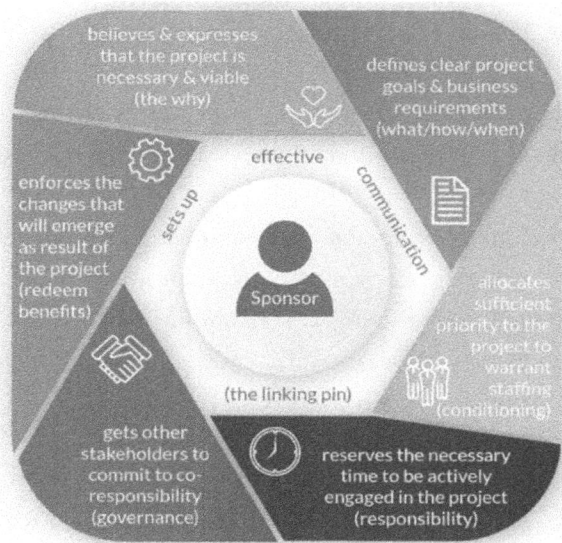

The desired prime responsibilities of a sponsor are:

Purpose
Believing and expressing that the project is necessary and viable. Being very clear on why the results of the project are so important for the business. (WHY)

> *"Your purpose explains what you are doing with your life. Your vision explains how you are living your purpose. Your goals enable you to realize your vision." ~ Bob Proctor*

Goals
Defining clear project goals and business requirements. Stating what the goals are, and how and when to achieve them. (WHAT, HOW, WHEN)

"If you aren't busy working on your own goals, you'll be working to achieve somebody else's goals." ~ Kevin Kruse

Conditions

Allocating sufficient priority to the project to warrant staffing of the project organization. Setting and complying to the conditions to make the project successful. (CONDITIONING)

Engagement

Reserving the necessary time to be actively engaged in the project. Explaining when you will be and want to be engaging with the project. (RESPONSIBILITY)

Governance

Getting other stakeholders to commit to co-responsibility. Arranging for what and when stakeholders will be held accountable. (GOVERNANCE)

Redemption

Enforcing the changes that will emerge as results of the project. Redeeming the results of the project into the organization. (REDEEM BENEFITS)

Communication

Setting up an effective communication process. Arranging who has to communicate with whom and about how, what, and when to communicate. (LINKING PIN)

At this point, you've made it through the main content of the Mindset Pillar. What follows is some action taking, bonus material, and a case study. Just because I didn't denominate them as main content doesn't mean these elements are not important. They reinforce the main content. So take some time and go through them. The case study will even give you an inside look at my first major success story that completely changed my life.

Your Mindset Call-for-Action: Get your mind in success mode

➔ Write down your Statement of Intent ⬅
"I will {objective} by {date} by {action}."

➔ Visualize and Declaim Your Golden Key to Success ⬅

Your Mindset Call-for-Reflection: Do you know your WHY?

Are You Vision Oriented?

Are your stakeholders well-informed and on the same page?

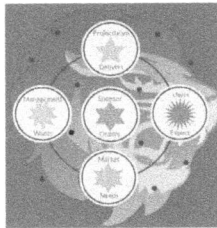

Are you motivated for the long term?

Bonus Chapter 1: "Ripple" your leadership

In this chapter, I address you as a leader with your values, with your WHY. For this, I use the teachings of the leadership expert Chris Hutchinson in his book *Ripple: A Field Manual for Leadership That Works*.

According to Hutchinson, leaders cannot be effective if they don't begin by understanding their own values, envisioning their personal futures, and recognizing their unique strengths and weaknesses.

In his book, Hutchinson demonstrates that true leadership is like skipping stones in a pond. He teaches that the secret to leadership is that the power is in the ripples, not in the stone. And stone-throwers simply can't set robust, long-lasting ripples in motion if they're not starting from a place of self-alignment. Hutchinson recommends three steps to get in alignment.

1. Decide on your values

Leaders who consciously and explicitly state their values lead from a place of clarity and empathy. Leaders who direct without such self-awareness tend to be defensive and unreceptive to the values of others.

To reveal what matters most to you, write down your top ten values. Now underline the top three. Finally, write out your understanding of how you are living (or not) those three values, including in your role as a business or project leader. Adjust your course as necessary.

2. Chart your own path

According to Hutchinson, the clarity of the end goal increases the clarity of the actions needed to achieve it. And nowhere is that truer than for leaders' personal visions for their own lives.

In his workshops, Hutchinson takes participants through a guided visualization. He tells them to close their eyes and picture their own memorial services three years from now. Then he asks: Who's attending the service? What do you want those people to remember and say about you? What do you want those people to carry on as your legacy?

Now ask yourself: How do I get from my reality of today to my hoped-for future? Start taking daily steps to get there.

3. Know where you're awesome

Are you often surprised or disappointed when others in your environment can't do (or see) the things you do? This is a sign that you don't know your own strengths, says Hutchinson. "When people unthinkingly see the abilities that come easily to them as not important or valuable, they are not recognizing—or even discrediting—their own strengths," he writes.

On the other hand, he adds, any strength overdone or used without thought can become a weakness. More is not always better.

To discover your sweet spot, Hutchinson advises making a list of things you find easy and fun. Circle or add anything that people often compliment you on. Validate by asking someone you trust to look at this list of strengths to see if they agree. Of course, third-party assessments such as DISC, Strengths Finder, and Workplace Motivators can also help you see and understand where you're awesome.

Truly effective organizational or team leadership starts with self-leadership, emphasizes Hutchinson. Next comes leadership of people and last, systems.

To put it in my own words, work on yourself first to make the biggest impact on your tribe and your operating environment.

Bonus Chapter 2: Overcome self-sabotage by using positive self-talk

Sometimes, we are our own worst enemy. We knock ourselves down and beat our emotions into the ground. Who needs enemies, when we are so accomplished at defeating ourselves.

It's high time to stop being so destructive to ourselves. Many people are masters at self-sabotage. Now is the time to become the best we can be at positive self-talk and take back the joy and happiness that we were born with.

While you may have tried affirmations before, perhaps you didn't have the success you wanted. There could be several reasons for that. For starters, if you do affirmations, it is not just repeating a phrase over and over. For affirmations to work, they must be specific to you, and they must be said with conviction. Stand in front of the mirror and state your affirmation with serious intent. You will see a major difference when you apply this simple technique.

Positive self-talk is different. In using positive self-talk, you need to do an assessment. Listen to yourself throughout the day and when you are making negative statements, pause and write them down.

For example, when you hear yourself say, "Ah, there is no way. I can't do this. It's too hard," quickly write that down in a notebook. Now underline the words, can't and it's too hard.

After a few days, take some time and sit down with your notebook. Review all the times you were engaging in negative self-talk. Think back to the situation and remember why you felt that way. Is there a behavior you were engaging in that you could change, and if so, would it lessen the desire to engage in negative talk? If the answer is yes, then start working on changing that behavior.

Now, look at the words you underlined. Those are the words that you need to eliminate from your vocabulary. They need to be deleted from your memory…forever.

Go back and look at the negative sentence and change it up a bit.
"Ah, this is interesting, it's not working yet. I am positive that I can find a way to make it work and make it fun."

There are many ways you could rewrite this sentence in your very own positive self-talk that reflects your personal situation.

As you work your way through identifying negative talk and replacing it with positive self-talk, you need to install an anchor.

An anchor is part of NLP…the language of our brain. Pick an anchor that suits your daily situation. If you work outside of the house, it should be something you can do, that people won't notice. When you hear the negative self-talk, mentally tell yourself to stop and then install a positive anchor. Here's how.

For instance, put your thumb against the pad of your baby finger and apply pressure. Repeating this, and then saying something positive, will cause you to stop the negative thought immediately and replace it with a positive one. Installing an anchor gives signals to our brains to pay attention and do what we want.

Now if you work from home, you can make it fun by slapping your hands together and yelling, "stop," each time you catch yourself doing the nasty self-talk.

As you master positive self-talk, you will see so many positive changes in your life. You will begin to sleep better, feel less stress, and smile more. Smiling more is very important. When you do that, it engages muscles, which activate positive chemicals in your body to make you feel great. That's why they say, "Laughter is the best medicine."

Case Study: How mindpower helped me achieve the most improbable

Here is my true story of how I achieved my first major and unforgettable personal success that completely changed my life. All just based on pure mindpower and knowing my why! This story has been published in the number-one bestseller *The Art and Science of Success, Volume 5, Proven Strategies From Today's Leading Experts.*

Setting the Scene

I was born and raised on a small island in the Caribbean, the first of ten children to be born in our family. Making ends meet in those postwar days, the late 1940s, was a big challenge to my parents—and everyone else, for that matter. Nevertheless, they urged us kids to go to school and learn to prepare for the future, a better future.

Being the eldest child, I had to set the example for the rest of the kids. I was determined to learn and be a role model, but I had a huge problem: I was a born stutterer. And I mean a profound stutterer. I could hardly get a word out of my mouth. This is a huge handicap for a child to cope with. My parents tried everything imaginable to help me get rid of this stuttering: medical specialists, shrinks, preachers, healers, voodoo priests, and even pebbles in my mouth.

Now, imagine me at school. Kids can be quite ruthless when they have somebody to pick on, and I was an easy target. It wasn't very uplifting for my self-esteem. When trying to produce a word, all I achieved was a red face from the effort it took to force the first sound of any word out of my mouth. My participation in any conversation was usually limited to silence. In the schoolyard and on the street, I had two choices: fight or withdraw from the scene. Being a rather skinny boy, I chose to withdraw. Needless to say, I didn't have many friends.

In the classroom, life was not much better. The written work was no problem. But my oral work was disastrous. Imagine me in front of the blackboard trying to explain a mathematical equation. To put it mildly, it didn't work. The teachers had a hard time with me. They couldn't treat me differently from my classmates, so they had to put me to the oral test from time to time, even knowing that I would fail. It was not a matter of my not knowing my stuff; I just couldn't express myself aloud. I learned to have several words with the same meaning available so that I could choose the one I might be able to pronounce at a given time. Because of this, I was even ahead of my classmates in terms of acquiring knowledge.

Then there was the fact that growing up in the Caribbean, we had not one, not even two, but four languages to learn. Again, the knowledge part wasn't the problem. On my native island we were raised to speak at least three languages at home and on the street, so we had a natural feeling for languages. But how does a stutterer read out loud? How does he recite a poem? How can he prove that his pronunciation is correct or not? That is a hell of a job for a stutterer like me. I knew exactly what I wanted to say and how I wanted to say it, but the words refused to roll out of my mouth.

Despite their frustration, my teachers were very understanding and compassionate toward me. They understood from my written work that I knew my stuff but just had a hard time with talking. We tried every trick in the book, from giving me my turn in the classroom unexpectedly to leaving it up to me when I felt ready to read, recite, or just talk. My teachers carefully weighed every word that I produced aloud to assess my oral achievements. At my oral final examinations, special measures were taken to accommodate me as much as possible so that my examiners could assess my knowledge of the languages. I went through an emotional hell those days, but I passed with flying colors at the age of 16 and was ready for college.

I got a scholarship from the government, and they appointed a mentor to guide me financially. Overnight I became a role model for all the kids in my community. That was an honor but also a burden. I couldn't afford to fail my family and my community. My whole neighborhood waved goodbye at the airport when I left my beautiful tropical island to study in the cold and rainy Netherlands. I was a teenager without the comfort of my family in a strange country where I knew nobody, all on my own, in a new environment, with new teachers, a new start, a new life. Would I succeed? I wanted to, but could I?

Wake-Up Call

In the Netherlands I enrolled in college, and, as you might guess, it was a disaster. The least of my problems was adjusting to my new environment. Being raised in the "hood" in a big family, I learned to adjust in order to survive. Here again, my disability in communicating orally with my professors and peers stood in the way of my success. I had questions to ask my professors, and I wanted to take part in the debates to show my skills and knowledge of the topic at hand. But the well-prepared words just didn't want to leave my mouth. At the end of that first year, I was not surprised that I was kicked out of college.

My financial mentor took me aside and told me to go back home because I didn't have what it took to make it at the college level. No way was I prepared to return home as a failure and disgrace my family and community. So I begged and negotiated with him to give me a second chance—in writing, of course. We finally agreed that I would take a psychological test to see if I had the potential to successfully complete college. If I failed the test, I would go back home, and if I passed the test, I would get a second chance. I knew I had the brains, so I was not surprised I passed the test and earned my second chance. We agreed that I would give it a shot in another city about a two-hour train journey away. This was my last chance, period. So I gathered my belongings and bought a one-way ticket to my new city of hope. Now what? This was my wake-up call!

Shortly after I took my seat, the train started to roll, giving me about two hours to get my act together. "John," I said to myself, "you have to believe in yourself, truly believe in yourself. No one else can help you. You have to do it on your own. You have to take the lead and take the lead now!" I guess I had to hit rock bottom before I could see the light. All it takes is the right mindset, determination, and action, and never giving up. There is just no other way.

There and then I decided that when I reached that new strange city, I would be another person. I would be able to talk my head off. Nobody would stand in my way. I would be the man in charge. I would take the lead to my destiny. I would take the lead to my success. I kept repeating that in my mind like a mantra. I imagined myself on stage talking to a large crowd of people, and how this crowd got carried away by my stirring speech. I knew I could do it. I knew the right words to use and how to say them; I just had to do it.

Success and Satisfaction

The train pulled into the station in my new city of hope. I straightened my back, stuck my head up in the air, and walked a bit cockily to the exit. This was a strange city to me, so I had to ask directions. When I did, the words just came rolling out of my mouth naturally. I was talking, no stuttering whatsoever. I did it! I did it! I did it! I was so happy; I said hello to everyone on my way to the bus. I only wanted to talk and keep on talking.

I felt reborn with the world at my feet. As improbable as it may seem, I did overcome stuttering on my own mindpower. If I can do that, I told myself, I can conquer anything. I just have to believe in myself, take the lead, and do it. From then on, I was unstoppable. I took any and every opportunity to talk and give speeches. In my college years, I joined all kinds of debating clubs. I graduated magna cum laude with a Master of Science degree in Information Systems. I gave speeches in different languages. In the communities where I lived, I was active in community groups, often as chairman. No matter where I was, my presence was noticed.

In all the assignments I had in my professional life, I took the lead. I reached the point where in almost any company I was in, I was expected to take the lead, to take the floor. Even while visiting friends in China, I was asked to hold a motivational speech in English to a group of franchise entrepreneurs. But in all humility, never forgetting where I came from, I always put the human factor at the core of all my undertakings. My tribe is sacred to me. Early in my career, I realized that communication was the main success factor.

My motto is Take the Lead with a Wink ;-). Relax, enjoy, and have fun while taking the lead. Then you will be not only a followed leader, but also a beloved leader. I believe that true leaders share their knowledge and experience with others so that they, in turn, can become true leaders themselves. Motivating and encouraging people in their endeavors to reach their goals is very rewarding and satisfying.

My mission is to help others take the lead to success and satisfaction.

Mindset on success! Now what?

Congratulations, you did it—you achieved your mindset in success mode! You're ready to offer your golden key to magnificence in leadership to the world. Start with your stakeholders.

Your next step is to find out how to nurture your tribe so they will gladly grant you success in your endeavor. The Grit Pillar will show you how to do that naturally. Now go "Grit" and take care of your stakeholders. They are waiting for you!

Pillar #2: Grit

"He ain't heavy, he's my brother."

Now that your mindset is in success mode, the Grit Pillar is the first pillar to profit from that state of mind. In the chapters falling under this pillar, you focus on creating relationships based on respect and understanding of the interests of each stakeholder. You draw the line, while you secure the collaboration of your stakeholders. You gladly take that responsibility on your shoulders. It's no burden because they are your people. The people who will grant you success. Go ahead and be their guide!

Chapter 2.0: Don't ask what they can do for you, ask what you can do for them!

I'm sure you've heard the term "What's in it for me?" somewhere along the line. It seems to be an almost natural reaction in these modern times when someone is expected to do anything. Yes, even if it's a part of their regular paid job. Whether you like it or not, it has become an inevitable part of life, and even more so in a business environment.

As a leader you would like to be able to anticipate that pressing question. It may be hidden in the silent posture of your stakeholder or team member, but you know it's there. It's the unspoken question you need to address if you want to get something done on your terms.

You can't ask your counterparts just out of the blue what they want or expect. To get to the bottom of that, you will have to build rapport with them to find out about their cherished interests. That's what the Grit Pillar is all about.

I will drill down into the relational core aspect of pragmatic leadership, the focus on creating a relationship with all parties involved. A relationship based on respect and understanding of the interests of each stakeholder. This relationship is the foundation for your success as a leader.

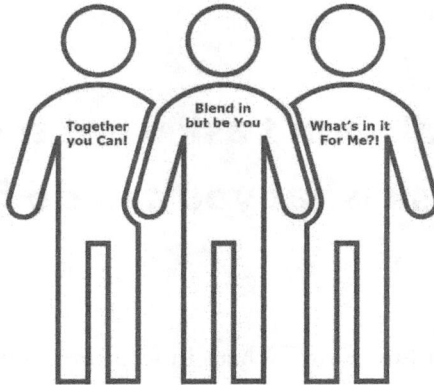

Know that you are dealing with human beings, people in various roles with a variety of interests, businesswise and personal. By building a relationship, you gain and give confidence and trust. So, you need to ensure an environment which grants you success; otherwise, you stand alone in your endeavor.

It's all about being the leader with grit. You draw the line, but you secure the collaboration of your stakeholders. And when you feel the going gets tough, get the tough going by embracing the evergreen saying: "He ain't heavy, he's my brother."

Let the following phrases guide you when you go through this pillar.

Achieving (business) goals … is all about people!

Blend in … but be yourself!

Together you can!

Communicate by all means, always and everywhere!

Listen, listen and listen!

The next chapter will illustrate what I've found to be the basic attitude qualities of a pragmatic leader with grit.

Chapter 2.1: The core attitude to blend in with your team and still be yourself (the 5 Ps)

Balancing the interests of all stakeholders and the pragmatic approach to the environment requires a leader with grit, and demands a certain core attitude. From surveying dozens of business, program, and project managers, and from my own experience, I came up with five basic attitude qualities for such a leader.

The pragmatic leader is like a chameleon. He adapts to his environment, but he remains himself. I characterize the attitude of such a leader by the so-called 5 Ps. Let me typify them one by one, concise but self-explanatory.

Positive in mindset

- Think challenge and solution, not problem and failure
- Build on the good, learn from the mistakes

Problems and failures will cross your path. Don't let them discourage you. Now that you're aware of them, learn from them so you can avoid them in the future. Each disadvantage conceals an advantage.

Pro-active in action

- Be alert and vigilant
- Anticipate—prevent rather than cure

See, hear, and feel what's going on around you. Stay ahead of unwanted surprises. Be safe rather than sorry.

Passionate in purpose

- Stand for your cause with heart and soul
- Remain credible in your enthusiasm

Be sure to know, live, and breathe your purpose (your WHY). That's your best insurance to be credible and trustworthy.

Pragmatic in execution

- Accept good is good enough
- Get more if possible

Surround yourself with the best specialists and let them do their thing at their best. But apply the 80/20 rule when it comes to balancing investment against profit.

Planning in delivery

- Plan short-term lasting milestones
- Control the process

This is the more rational part of leadership where brain prevails over passion. The traditional manager in you takes over. Nevertheless, make sure you define viable milestones. Viable meaning feasible milestones with their own purpose or value for your business goals.

By applying these attitude qualities, you will be well equipped to be a pragmatic leader with confidence, credibility, and persuasiveness. Practice this behavior long enough and it will become your new habit. A habit that is bound to make you a successful pragmatic leader.

The next chapter will elaborate on why it is advantageous to focus on the interests of your stakeholders.

Chapter 2.2: Why to focus on the interests of all stakeholders

More and more business projects tend to cross organizational boundaries and meet conflicting interests. Stakeholder management provides for an open dialogue between stakeholders, based on mutual respect for each other's ideas and values, and aimed to achieve the best possible viable results.

A stakeholder is anyone who has a justifiable interest in the project. So you can't choose your stakeholders at random, but you can determine the most important ones to deal with. What's the stakeholder's position in the project's force field? What's their influence? What's their interest in the results? What benefit will they gain from the project? Can you depend on them or do you still have to work on their support?

Position, knowledge, attitude and behavior of the stakeholders will determine how to deal with them. It comes down to having and applying a communication strategy that resonates with and appeals to their interests. This can be on content, the process, and the relationship.

To get your stakeholders all lined up for your cause, you will have to know their interests, both businesswise and personal. They all have different roles in your project and therefore different interests to satisfy so you can succeed in your endeavor.

The stakeholders' direct business interests are quite obvious by the roles they play in your project. But that is just the tip of the iceberg. What really matters is their indirect business interests and their personal interests.

Your job is to get and keep all these interests in balance to keep the stakeholders happy and committed. Indirect business interests and personal interests can often make the difference between success and failure.

"To lead, you have to care. You can't fake it." ~ Kevin Kruse

Interesting indirect business-related questions are, for instance, who is the client of the client, who is the customer of the customer, are there external or internal suppliers or both. It's like the question behind the question. Knowing the answer to these kinds of questions can help you understand your stakeholders' position.

Everyone has that aching question in their mind "What's in it for me?" And you should be aware of that and get to the bottom of it. Remember it's all about human beings with their needs, dreams, and wishes. Maybe they just are looking for a raise or a promotion. Maybe they want to secure their job. Or maybe they desire an increase in sales or production. These are all business-related issues, direct or indirect.

Personal interests can also influence the commitment and performance of stakeholders. Things like family matters, financial matters, neighborhood matters, you get the drift. Lend a listening ear—that can perform miracles.

The bottom line here is to be concerned with the interests—business and personal—of all your stakeholders to keep the ball rolling your way.

In the next chapter, I will show you how you can put communication to work strategically.

Chapter 2.3: How to put communication to work strategically

Organizations are always on the innovation streak due to new customer demands, increasing competition, and changing legislation. Nevertheless, organizations operate in the now and are not always eager to change. Often projects get initiated apart from the standing organization with its limited resources. Before you know it there is a conflict of interest that leads to an "us" versus "them" discussion.

Support is essential to realize change, and communication is key to obtain that support. Directed communication with stakeholders is crucial. They have to live through the project, talk about it, and promote it. The importance of the project will become visible on all levels. Here is where using communication strategically comes in handy. First, you need information about the change scope and the stakeholders to make up the change story. And once you have the change story, you can finally share it strategically. Here are the steps involved in this process.

1. Change Ambition

The goal here is defining the scope for the change. What are the turnaround times, the budgets, and the impact on the organization? How are human resources distributed? Whose tasks are affected by the project results? What resistance can be expected and from whom? How can the resistance be countered effectively? Who will own the results of the project in the standing organization? The result of this step is a sharp picture of the scope of the project, the conditions, and the responsibilities.

2. Stakeholder Analysis

This step is about finding the relevant stakeholders. Who has a business interest in the project and who can influence the outcome? Where interest and influence coincide determines whether we are dealing with a strategical supporter or opponent. Both will need your devoted attention. For matters of governance we must agree upon who has to be informed, consulted, or involved concerning the project and the change.

The result is a clear force field stakeholder matrix and a clear governance agreement.

3. Drafting the Change Story

Here you are going to find the right change story to address the concerns of all stakeholders. In other words, this is the story behind the reasoning of the change that appeals to the stakeholders. This involves finding out what matters to the stakeholders, the arguments that mean the most to them. To do that you form a small, involved group of stakeholders to brainstorm about the impact of the project and the means of communication. You are looking for their basic concerns and the wording that goes with them. You are seeking commitment and basic support to get the ball rolling.

The result is a set of core messages that represent the change and that appeal to the stakeholders. The change story.

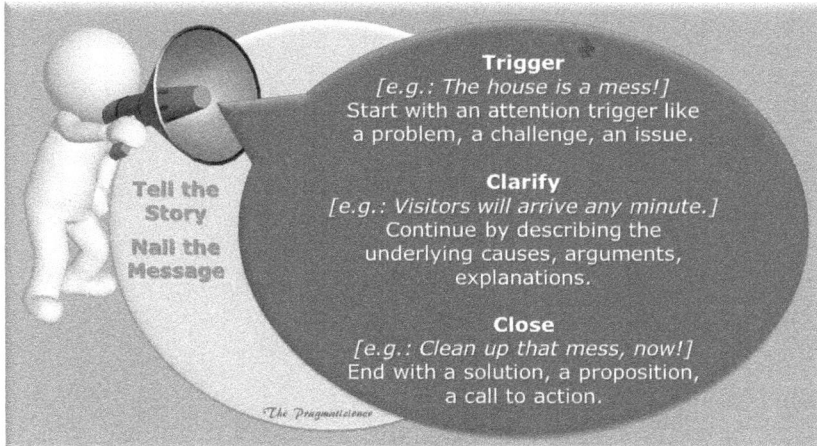

Tell the Story
Nail the Message

Trigger
[e.g.: The house is a mess!]
Start with an attention trigger like
a problem, a challenge, an issue.

Clarify
[e.g.: Visitors will arrive any minute.]
Continue by describing the
underlying causes, arguments,
explanations.

Close
[e.g.: Clean up that mess, now!]
End with a solution, a proposition,
a call to action.

The Pragmaticlance

4. Spreading the Change Story

Now you use the messages in the change story for the directed communication about the project. You mold the story to suit the means of communication, and you appoint a storyteller that fits best for the audience undergoing the story. The tailormade story is presented naturally and supported by visuals. The objective is that the audience recognizes the change and can live through the change. Monitoring the effect of the communication efforts is also part of the job and includes adjusting communication means and content if and when necessary.

The result is an extended understanding and recognition of the change and its effect, and managed stakeholder expectations.

Bottom Line

Change is meant to benefit the organization, and organizations consists of people. People can only be reached, heard, and influenced through communication—by explaining patiently and by giving the change a human voice. Successful communication is about seducing, connecting, storytelling. That's what strategical communication is all about.

The next chapter is about securing the collaboration of your stakeholders.

Chapter 2.4: How to secure collaboration with your tribe (the 2 Cs)

Coping with the human environment of your endeavor is all about communication and commitment, the 2 Cs. Commitment can only be attained by good communication. At the same time, commitment can make communication more efficient.

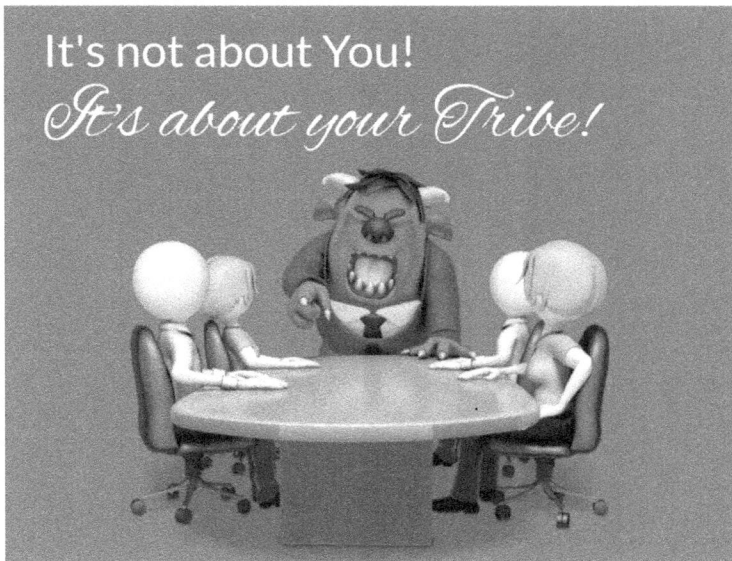

"Employee engagement is the emotional commitment an employee has to the organization and its goals." ~ Kevin E. Kruse

1. Communication

Communication is the medium of choice to determine the interests of the stakeholders, but also to clarify where you stand. All forms of communication are permissible and even desirable: meetings, conversations in the coffee corner, at the bar, on the golf course, one on one, you name it!

The informal discussions need not always be about the business, but can also be about home, the kids, sports, etc. Of course, you take part in all these avenues of communication, but perhaps your most important contribution is to listen, listen, and listen even more.

2. Listening

Because listening is so important, I'll elaborate a little more on this topic. If you could boil down one key ingredient to be a people person—in this case, a people-centered leader—it would be to listen. In general, people are too wrapped up in themselves and don't listen.

When you become a good listener, you will stand out from the crowd and people will take notice of this personal trait. More people will approach you and, in many cases, they won't even know why. It's not as if you announce to the world, "I am a good listener. Come talk to me." It will happen naturally because you are listening.

Many people mistake listening with giving advice. That is not always a good idea. In fact, unless you are a counselor, or you are an expert on the subject of the conversation, you want to avoid advice as much as possible. You don't want to give people bad advice that if followed, will lead to a difficult situation.

Listening involves hearing what the other person has to say completely and then interpreting what is being said. If you need to respond, you can acknowledge what was said. Some people like to repeat what the other person says after he or she says it. That can be awkward for the person talking, but it is helpful to ensure you understand what was said.

You can also follow up with words of encouragement or empathy, depending on how the conversation is going. That is different from offering advice. You are letting the other person know you heard what he or she said and responding accordingly.

In most conversations, one person will speak about himself or herself. When the person finishes, the other person will speak about himself or herself. That is a common form of conversation, but neither party is truly listening to the other. Take an interest in the other parties and let the conversation be about them. You will have plenty of time in other conversations to make it about you. To further the conversation, ask questions about what was said. That shows you are interested. People love to talk about themselves. Let them do this.

Listening is a skill. Just like anything else, it takes practice. When you become a good listener you will become more of a people person by using this skill to its fullest.

Use the obtained information not only in the interest of the project, but also in the personal interest of the stakeholders. It's all about people, and if you as a leader can help the stakeholders in any way, this will also benefit your endeavor!

3. Commitment

Commitment starts by fostering understanding of each other's views and ideas. By gaining an understanding of each other's perspective everyone will be more inclined to see the similarities, bridge the differences, help each other and dedicate themselves to the ultimate goal.

Gaining commitment is a process. Be aware of the different phases of the commitment perception of your stakeholders. Then you can recognize them and deal with them properly.

Phase	Perception
Denial	Changes never happen around here
Resistance	They try this from time to time—just ignore it
Acceptance	Seems like a sensible plan
Exploration	What's in it for me?
Commitment	It will help me—what's next?

The bottom line for your stakeholder or team member is always: What's in it for me!

4. Key Players

Finding and involving key figures will contribute significantly to a commitment to the project. Key figures are not necessarily the business executives. Key people include specialists, authority figures, advocates, but also opponents. These are all people with a certain group of supporters. When you mobilize these types of key figures, their supporters go along. Get the key figures to take responsibility!

Make clear agreements with the parties concerned. Make SMART agreements, at least measurable ones. This way you create win-win situations. The parties then see that their interests are also secured. That will strengthen your authority as a leader.

The next chapter is about mastering your communication skills.

Chapter 2.5: How to master your communication skills

If you want to be an expert communicator, you need to be effective at all points in the communication process—from "sender" to "receiver" and back to "sender"—and you must be comfortable with the different channels of communication—face-to-face, voice-to-voice, written, etc.

When you communicate with someone else, you each follow certain steps of the communication process. You, as the source of the communication, plan and craft it into a message, and deliver it through a channel. The receiver interprets the message, and, in one way or another, gives you feedback on understanding or a lack of understanding.

"People may hear your words, but they feel your attitude."
~ John C. Maxwell

By understanding the steps in the process, you can become more aware of your role in it, recognize what you need to do to communicate effectively, anticipate problems before they occur, and improve your overall ability to communicate effectively.

1. Planning the Message

What is your message? Why this message? Who is your audience? How will you send your message? How will you get feedback?

Before you start communicating, take a moment to figure out what you want to say, and why. Keep it simple and to the point.

- Understand your objective. Why are you communicating?
- Understand your audience. With whom are you communicating? What do they need to know?
- Plan what you want to say, and how you'll send the message.
- Seek feedback on how well your message was received.

2. Crafting the Message

Is your message clear and concise? Are you choosing the right words for the audience you are addressing? Are you taking in account the difference between spoken and written language?

When you know what you want to say, decide exactly how you'll say it. Also consider how you think your audience will perceive your message. Effective communication means:

- Understanding what you truly want to say.
- Anticipating the reaction to your message.
- Choosing words and body language that allow your audience to really hear what you're saying.

With written communication, make sure that what you write will be perceived the way you intend. Words on a page generally have no emotion. When writing, take time to:

- Review your style.
- Avoid jargon or slang.
- Check your grammar and punctuation.
- Check for tone, attitude, nuance, and other subtleties.
- Familiarize yourself with your company's writing policies.

Consider using pictures, charts, and diagrams. "A picture speaks a thousand words."

Also, whether you speak or write your message, consider the cultural context. If there's potential for misunderstanding due to cultural or language barriers, address these issues in advance.

3. Delivering the Message

What is the most effective communication channel for your message and your audience? Will you speak or write your message?

Along with crafting the message, you need to choose the best communication channel to deliver it. Will you speak or write your message? You want to be efficient, and yet make the most of your communication opportunity.

When you determine the best way to deliver a message, consider:

- The sensitivity and emotional content of the subject.
- How easy it is to communicate detail.
- The receiver's preferences.
- Time constraints.
- The need to ask and answer questions.

4. Interpreting the Message

Active listening, undivided attention to the speaker. Empathic listening, understand the emotions and the body language of the speaker.

It can be easy to focus on speaking; however, to be a great communicator, you also need to step back, let the other person talk, and just listen. That doesn't mean that you should be passive. Listening is hard work, which is why effective listening is called active listening.

To listen actively, give your undivided attention to the speaker:

- Look at the person.
- Pay attention to his or her body language.
- Avoid distractions.
- Nod and smile to acknowledge points.
- Occasionally think back about what the person has said.
- Allow the person to speak, without thinking about what you'll say next.
- Don't interrupt.

Empathic listening also helps to interpret a message accurately. To understand a message fully, you have to interpret the emotions and underlying feelings the speaker is expressing. That is where an understanding of body language can be useful.

5. Getting Feedback

Getting feedback verbally and through body language. Asking questions and repeating the answers in your own words to verify your understanding.

You need feedback, because without it, you can't be sure that your audience has understood your message. Sometimes feedback is verbal, and sometimes it's not. Ask questions and listen carefully. However, feedback through body language is perhaps the most important source of clues to the effectiveness of your communication. By watching the facial expressions, gestures, and posture of the person you're communicating with, you can spot confidence, defensiveness, agreement, understanding, interest, engagement, truthfulness, and so on.

As a speaker, understanding your listener's body language can give you an opportunity to adjust your message and make it more understandable, appealing, or interesting.

As a listener, body language can show you more about what the other person is saying. You can then ask questions to ensure that you have, indeed, understood each other.

Feedback can also be formal. If you're communicating something really important, it is worth asking questions to the people you're talking to and making sure that they've understood fully. And if you're receiving this sort of feedback, repeat it in your own words to verify your understanding.

In the next chapter, I will show you how to thrive by nurturing your team.

Chapter 2.6: How to thrive by nurturing your tribe

As a leader you also are a bridge builder and team builder. One of your toughest tasks is to get and keep others motivated, especially your tribe. Just shouting that they have to do something is not usually an effective method. It may work in the short-term, but over the long run, it fails. You thrive best by nurturing your tribe.

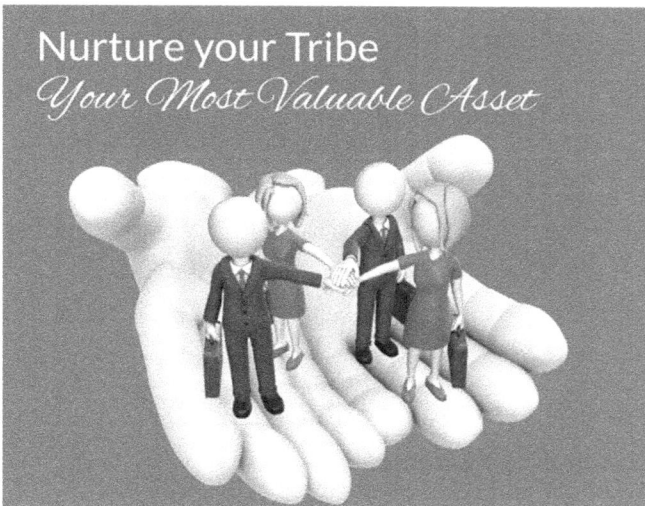

"Leaders must be close enough to relate to others, but far enough ahead to motivate them." ~ John C. Maxwell

Here are some useful tips to get you going on the tribe nurturing trip.

1. Set an Example

It is much easier to get someone to do what you ask when you first are willing to do it yourself. The people you are leading may not know how to do what you ask. When you show them, they immediately know they can come to you when they get stuck. Even if you don't know how to do something that you ask others to do, being there to try and help solve the problem can go a long way.

2. Be Passionate

If you love what you do, people will pick up on that. It will be much easier for them to take your lead when they see you are passionate. You become a kind of cheerleader and people will catch on to your enthusiasm. By contrast, you won't be able to convince too many people if you are not passionate.

3. Know What Others Want

When you can push the right buttons in people by learning what they want, they will follow you to no end. That is going to require truly listening to people to discover what they are looking to accomplish. When you have that knowledge, you can find ways to make sure people get what they need. They will appreciate receiving this from you.

4. Encourage Others' Strengths

When you know about peoples' abilities, make sure you let others know, too. Encouraging is a great booster in their confidence, and it will get them to want to do what you ask. They will be proud that you have championed them, and they'll respect you for it.

5. Let People See the Answers for Themselves

When you set up an environment where people learn about the solutions on their own, there is very little need to motivate them. They will come to the right discoveries and will know what needs to get done. That is by far the easiest way to get others to act.

6. Try to See from Others' Perspectives

Walk a mile in another's shoes, as the saying goes. When you know where others are coming from, it will be easier to motivate them by getting in sync with their personalities. Trying to force others to your way of thinking is much less effective.

At this point, you've made it through the main content of the Grit Pillar. What follows is some action taking, bonus material, and a case study. Just because I didn't denominate them as main content doesn't mean they are not important. They reinforce the main content. So take some time and go through them. The case study is a typical illustration of how focusing on the interests of stakeholders can save your project.

Your Grit Call-for-Action:
Rank your communication skills

➜ Use this Communication Skills Self-Assessment to rate your skills. ⬅

Assessment Procedure	Rating Table
1. Rate each process step on a scale of 1 to 5 (see Rating Table).	1 = Very Poor
	2 = Poor
2. Take note of your results.	3 = Mediocre
3. Take action to improve any underrated process steps.	4 = Strong
4. Re-assess in due time.	5 = Very Strong
5. Celebrate your progress!	

Assessment

Communication Step	Requirements to meet	Rating
Planning the Message	What is your message? Why this message? Who is your audience? How will you send your message? How will you get feedback?	
Crafting the Message	Is your message clear and concise? Are you choosing the right words for your audience?	

	Are you distinguishing between spoken and written language?	
Delivering the Message	What is the most effective communication channel for your message and your audience? Will you speak or write your message?	
Interpreting the Message	Active listening, undivided attention to the speaker. Empathic listening, understand the emotions and the body language of the speaker.	
Getting Feedback	Getting feedback verbally and through body language. Asking questions and repeating the answers in your own words to verify your understanding.	

Your Grit Call-for-Reflection: Do you know your environment?

Are you aware of your stakeholders' interests?

Are you listening enough to your stakeholders?

Do you know who your key players are?

Bonus Chapter 1: How to save time without losing control

The ideas I'm about to put to you are some of the ways high-level leaders succeed. Some of the ideas can be incorporated immediately, while others, such as the ones regarding software or apps…will require a bit of research and decision making.

1. Set your goals

Are you 100 percent clear on what your project goals are? You need to get your new project off to a flying start. Or if you have been in business for a while and have been experiencing issues, it may be due to not seeing things crystal clear. Consider having a self-improvement goal as part of your business goals. Self-improvement will strengthen the other areas of your goal setting. Get a mentor or coach who has the experience in the areas of self-confidence, self-esteem or creating a new mindset around achieving success in business.

You need to set specific goals and keep track of everything. If you want to be a high-functioning, successful leader, think about tracking everything daily in a special spreadsheet.

Stop your internal negative dialogue. When you have lofty business goals, sometimes you end up talking yourself out of something that if you stuck to it…would be ultimately successful. Hannibal saw the mountains and said, "We will either find a way or make one." Leading thousands of soldiers and elephants over a mountain range, Hannibal had an extremely positive mental image of himself.

Have a great idea? If you start to balk, take the first few actions and as you see success, put your foot on the accelerator and get up to speed. Internal negative dialogue destroys dreams and ambition. You can overcome that and build an amazing business.

2. Define the tasks to achieve those goals

When you have a business idea and want to either start it or add it to your existing business, you need to define your tasks. Here is where you put on your strategic thinking hat and write out the who, what, where of your tasks.

Who will help you? Do you have a team already that has the skills to get the new business up and running, then turn it into a profit? What exactly is the business? Make a business plan. Add mind maps. Where will you conduct this business? Decide if you have enough space. Do you need to upgrade? How long will it take to get this business off the ground?

Writing out the tasks and adding time-to-completion dates will help save time and achieve your goals.

3. Draw up a plan

Everyone needs a plan. And a true leader always creates the best plan possible, while putting together an amazing team. It is a case of knowing the strengths and weaknesses of the team members. With that knowledge, you can decide the best person for a task, set the deadlines, the goals and of course the rewards. With technology today, project management tools help the leader keep everything on track.

4. Eliminate distractions, useless tasks or time wasters

As a leader, it's essential that you eliminate distractions. One of the best things that you can do for yourself is hiring a personal assistant. A quality you want to look for is their ability to say, "No," in a polite yet firm way. Personal assistants can either advise people that you won't attend a meeting or go and represent you. Virtual assistants are now available. You can hire a company that has a team of VAs to take over all the requests you get.

Filtering meeting requests is another way to stop the interruptions. Find out ahead of time what the meeting entails and the sort of questions that need to be answered. With this information, you can decide if it is an absolute necessity for you to be there. You can say no or decide which team member is best suited to take your place.

As a leader, you may want to adopt the mindset of some of the toppers in the field. There are leaders who assign weights to requests and possible time wasters. If a request isn't hitting an 8 out of 10 on the scale, then simply say no. Or if you get a request for a meeting or a proposal and you don't do a mental backflip of joy, then it's just a no-go situation.

5. Automate tasks

There are many cool tools and software available for tasks that can be automated, saving you a lot of time and money. Do your due diligence to find the right tool for the right task.

6. Delegate tasks

Delegate any task that doesn't need your unique skills or added value. Value your own time, and you will see that outsourcing or having a virtual assistant is extremely cheap compared to executing certain tasks on your own.

As a leader, failure to delegate may mean the end of your endeavor. No one wants to start over again, especially due to a simple mistake. In the successful leader's mind, there is a small compartment that understands micromanaging employees equals failure.

Hiring a virtual assistant is very easy these days. With a team, even a small one to start and then to grow, a virtual or personal assistant can manage and direct that team, while you focus on the big picture.

7. Focus on YOUR tasks

Focus on the tasks that will help you achieve your goals and that require your unique added value.

Finally, we come down to an absolute must for any leader. Focus! Without being able to focus on what is truly important, you will self-sabotage your future. Let's get busy and talk about the ultimate focus for leaders.

Have you ever heard the expression, "Well he or she is not the sharpest knife in the drawer"? That certainly does not and will not apply to you. You are already sharp; now you just have to hone that sharp focus. Some call it laser focus due to the cutting ability of a laser.

All leaders start with a business plan. They might have a simple one that they put together themselves, or they have a skilled writer put their plan together.

The leader's main focus here is to get funding. How can they mess this up? By allowing their minds to take over and start playing an internal negative dialogue. Before any leader heads off to a sponsor, they need to be crystal clear in their mind about what they want and when they want it.

Hesitation or anxiety over being turned down for funding can derail you. Focus instead on the merits of your business and your abilities to make your venture successful. Sponsors can smell fear a mile away. Have a clear vision in your mind as you walk through that door.

Since your business plan is complete, you need to focus on the tasks at hand. Write out clear goals in a 90-day framework and then break them down into smaller time chunks. What are you going to focus on in the first 30 days?

You can only achieve a laser-like focus if your physical and mental health is at peak. You need to eat properly throughout the day. Stay hydrated and eat a lot of fruit. Of course, you need to exercise to reduce stress and clear your mind.

Getting the proper amount of sleep is paramount to great focus. To sleep well, clear your mind of all negative thoughts and do some empowering affirmations before bedtime. Your brain will work on these powerful affirmations while you sleep so that you wake up refreshed.

Have a cold shower when you wake up early in the morning. That will help you to get focused on the day, and you can do some deep breathing exercises before getting dressed.

Successful leaders take Brian Tracy's book, *Eat that Frog*, as gospel truth. In that regard, many of them tackle the biggest, hardest task first thing. They come at it with laser focus and complete it. Doing this sets up their entire day because they WON, first thing in the morning. Their mindset is, "That is crossed off. I am unstoppable."

Here is a cool concept used by some entrepreneurs. It's a ranking of numbers. They focus on a task and they have a timeframe that they work from. It could be five minutes or ten minutes. They ask themselves, "Will this matter in five minutes, five hours, five weeks, five months or five years?" If the answer is yes, then that task is very important, and they focus on doing everything required to complete that task.

You can completely lose focus if you concern yourself about the competition. It's important to focus on your business because you have no control over what others are doing.

Take the time to develop a laser-like focus on your tasks and ultimately your business or project. The rewards will be more than worth it.

Bonus Chapter 2: How to deal with difficult people

When you are a people-centered leader, you're going to often come across difficult people. These are people who won't yield for any reason. They are unreasonable and will likely complain about everything. How can you deal with these people?

1. Apathetic behavior

Some people become apathetic in their situations. They used to care but felt something or someone along the way just didn't care. Their reasoning is, if others don't care, why should they? When this is the case, you can usually break down the barriers by getting to the root of the problem. Ask questions of this person. Find out what it is that is causing them not to care anymore.

2. Bad attitude

For others who simply have a bad attitude, you have to handle this situation more delicately. The one thing you don't want to do is give in to them so readily. Sometimes, people will acquiesce to those who bark the loudest. But you should only let them have their way if their solution is the correct one, not just because they are barking.

3. Alternative solutions

One of the main tactics in dealing with difficult people is to have alternative solutions. For instance, if someone complains that a particular solution won't work, first ask why. If they come up with a valid reason, then offer alternatives. If they continue to shoot down every suggestion you produce, ask them to come up with a solution of their own.

4. Difficult sponsors

Dealing with difficult sponsors is a tougher situation, as the sponsor has the upper hand. Sometimes, it can be a temporary situation where the sponsor is dealing with personal problems. If you can get him or her to talk about it, you may be able to diffuse the situation.

5. Consider retreating

Some sponsors are unreasonable or incompetent. It is just their nature, and there's not much you will be able to do or say to change that. In this case, you may have to consider retreating from the project.

6. Get to the cause

When dealing with difficult people, you have to try to get to the cause of their behavior. It's only then that you will be able to effectively determine whether you can help the person overcome some obstacle that is making him or her difficult. It will also let you determine if you need to move on from that person or not.

Case Study: How focusing on the interests of stakeholders saved my project

The Client

Leading internationally operating paper company with headquarters in Sweden. Sales and customer service departments are located in the major European countries to serve their customers in the local language and customs. Corporate language is English. Their USP for this case study is servicing their customers through short lines of communication in the local language and cultural setting.

The Challenge

The board of directors wants to cut operational costs by centralizing sales and customer service in one geographical location while maintaining their USP. The board chose Amsterdam in the Netherlands.

That entails setting up an international multilingual and multicultural call center with all its technical and personnel challenges, and no extra costs for their customers. All to be fully operational within a year.

A not unimportant challenge was the fact that the locally residing employees didn't like this plan. Despite being loyal employees, they were not eager to be separated from their families and cultural environment for longer periods of time. Moving to another country was no option, especially for those with school-age children.

Nevertheless, the board persisted in following through with their plan. They went looking for a project manager in the Netherlands to set up the desired call center in Amsterdam. In their selection procedure, they selected me due to my track record in IT and communication projects. That I understand and speak five languages was an additional benefit.

My assignment was to set up the call center in the technical sense, working smoothly across the country borders of telecommunication. The linguistic and cultural aspects were not to be my concern. They considered that to be an internal company issue. Locally operating sales and customer service staff members would be flown in for the testing phase of the project. I reported to the utility manager, who was my formal project sponsor.

My Solution

I had enough experience with similar IT and communication projects. The technical aspects of the call center were not that difficult to tackle. The call forward function was the most challenging technical aspect—making sure that the calling customer was always connected to a native speaking staff member within three ringtones. For that issue, I recruited a telecom subcontractor with whom I have worked before. After all, I was chosen because of that experience and my contacts in that field.

In my opinion, the success of the whole mission was fully dependent on the participation of the future employees of the call center. That became quite visible when the first local staff members were flown in to organize the offices in the call center building. You could feel the tension in the air.

As I could often speak to them in their native language, I could rapidly establish a good rapport with many of the foreign staff members. That way I learned that they were never involved in the decision-making process to centralize sales and customer support. They were just told that the move would take place within one year.

These were the people I needed to test the workings of the call center I would deliver. They were already frustrated by this move of the board and were not in the mood to be collaborative. So it was in my best interest, even though it wasn't my primary responsibility, to find a way to gain their trust and unbiased participation in the project.

Not being formally accountable for their actions, I could only appeal to the employees on a personal level. I decided to listen to their grievances and talk to them about their home situation, lending them an ear and a shoulder. That on its own gave them some comfort and relief.

In the meantime, I also managed to establish a good, even friendly relationship with my project sponsor and the general manager of the staff members. The general manager also noticed my friendly connection with the foreign staff members. I gradually maneuvered myself into the role of mediator. For me, that was a win-win position without requiring me to be accountable.

The foreign staff members felt recognized by management in their grievances. They even received some extra secondary benefits. Management saw a decrease in tension on the work floor and a more cooperative workforce. And I had a team of staff members who were willing to go that extra mile for me to make the call center a success in the given timeline.

The Results

The desired call center in Amsterdam was delivered fully operational in the given timeline within a year.

Management has a better understanding of the grievances of the foreign staff members.

Foreign staff members are inclined to be more cooperative in achieving this specific goal of the board.

I got a farewell party from the management with a large bottle of vodka and a pair of Swedish skates as a gift. I guess they were pleased with my performance.

You and your tribe are ready to take off! Not enough?

Sure, you're all pumped up for success and you secured the collaboration of your stakeholders. They are ready and eager to follow your lead. They are ready to go for it. They can already taste the sweetness of success.

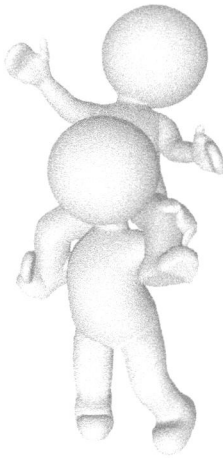

But what about your operational environment? Don't you want to know how to get that under control? Your next stop is the Grip Pillar, which is designed to help you read, profile, and gain control of your operational circumstances. Take "Grip" and expand your reach of influence and control!

Pillar #3: Grip

"About influence and influencing!"

At this point, you have your mindset in success mode, and you secured the collaboration of the individual stakeholders. In this pillar, you expand your reach and profile your environment to get in control of your operational circumstances. This is about influence and influencing. Time to get in control!

Chapter 3.0: Read the environment and get in control

Gaining rapport with your stakeholders and team members is crucial but still not enough to secure your success as a leader. Just as important are the circumstances under which you have to work. Each endeavor or project has its specific circumstances to take into account.

Does the term "Location, location, location!" ring a bell? It's a simplification for what I mean by environment, but it points in the right direction. Not only the physical environment can influence your success, but even more so the organizational, cultural, and political operating conditions. You will have to deal with all these aspects to be successful in your endeavor.

I will zoom in on the situational core aspect of pragmatic leadership, getting a grip on the specific environmental circumstances of a project. In addition, I'll address tailoring the leader's approach to deal with these circumstances and getting the right stakeholders to do the right things in the right order to achieve the desired results.

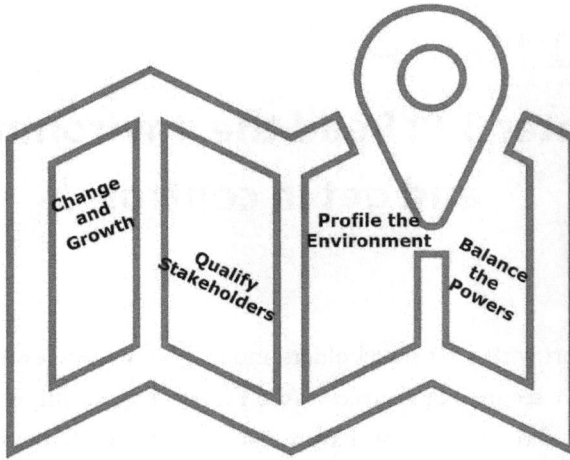

While we're at it, I want to draw your attention to a much-overlooked aspect when it comes to projects, or any business endeavor for that matter. Coping with this aspect can mean the difference between success and failure.

Each project result aims in principle to bring about change and growth in the organization. A fitting adage for this would be "Improving, Changing, Anchoring."

With each new project, we try to typify the project to get a clear picture to determine the best possible approach for success. Some relevant questions come to mind.

- Does the project meet the conditions for change and growth?
- What is the delivery strategy for the project?
- What about the possible phasing of the execution of the project?
- What about the maturity of the organization where the project is embedded?
- How about the power balance between stakeholders?

Time and again I'm surprised to discover how often these questions can appear to be eye-openers for many a sponsor.

I will tackle the topics of those questions using strategic and tactical tools to help you read and control the environment you operate in. This is powerful but also sensitive stuff, so use properly and with integrity.

The big takeaway from this pillar is that reading the environment and getting in control is about influence and influencing!

In the next chapter, I will dig into the business of change and growth.

Chapter 3.1: The business of change and growth

In business, it's all about change and growth to survive in a competitive world. So as a leader, you are in the business of change and growth. To fully implement change, an understanding of the components of systemic reform requires experience, people skills, and extreme patience.

Knoster, T. (1991), in a presentation to The Association for Severely Handicapped (TASH) Conference, introduced a Managing Complex Change Model that has several components. Knoster suggested that when the components of vision, consensus, skills, incentives, resources and action plan are collectively inherent in the system, then change will likely take place. But if any one of the components is missing, then the "Change Process" may be inhibited or may not take root.

Vision	Consensus	Skills	Incentives	Resources	Action Plan	**Change**
-	Consensus	Skills	Incentives	Resources	Action Plan	**Confusion**
Vision	-	Skills	Incentives	Resources	Action Plan	**Sabotage**
Vision	Consensus	-	Incentives	Resources	Action Plan	**Anxiety**
Vision	Consensus	Skills	-	Resources	Action Plan	**Resistance**
Vision	Consensus	Skills	Incentives	-	Action Plan	**Frustration**
Vision	Consensus	Skills	Incentives	Resources	-	**Treadmill**

Vision

The organization's mission, vision, and goals, and how to achieve them.

Consensus

Consensus by all parties concerning tasks, jurisdictions, responsibilities, and the organization of activities.

Incentives

The culture of how all concerned interact with each other. "What's in it for me?"

Skills

Necessary skills and competencies for all concerned to deal with their tasks.

Resources

Operational means like finance, IT, communication, and other facilities.

Action Plan

Plans on how and when to execute the tasks and activities.

Cause and consequence in a nutshell:

Component	Ensures	Or else
Vision	Clarity	Confusion
Consensus	Commitment	Sabotage
Incentives	Acceptance	Anxiety
Skills	Confidence	Resistance
Resources	Enthusiasm	Frustration
Action Plan	Stability	Treadmill

A unique feature of Knoster's model for change is its surgical approach. In assessing the condition and climate of an organization, this model offers a potential remedy by identifying the symptom and then restoring the missing component. Quite often leaders may sense what is wrong, but do not understand how to resolve or determine the root of the problem.

As an example, if you sense or anticipate sabotage as a symptom from within the organization, then the ability to work through consensus through collaboration is paramount. If there is a high level of resistance, then you need to identify the incentives and determine what will personally motivate an individual to change. Sometimes the problems are so severe that multiple missing components have created a hostile environment that is difficult to sort through.

Although the model may appear to be simple, it is a powerful tool to connect the symptom with the components of change. Unless a leader can connect with the people of the organization through empathic listening, he or she will never understand the emotion behind the concerns. Developing this trust through relationship building may draw out the essential missing component. Then the change process may continue to develop and help the organization arrive at the desired results.

This Knoster Model fits in perfectly with my core aspect approach to pragmatic leadership.

Situational 'Strategy & Structure'		Relational 'People & Culture'		Rational 'Resources & Results'	
Vision	Consensus	Skills	Incentives	Resources	Action Plan

Use this model to set your components right and adjust them when necessary by addressing the symptoms you encounter on your path. To do that, connect with your stakeholders through empathic listening to establish trust.

The next chapter is about reading and profiling your operating environment.

Chapter 3.2: How to profile your operating environment

Every endeavor or project has its specific characteristics. They eventually define the best way to deliver the intended results. That means the best delivery strategy and phasing in that particular organizational environment. Here I provide the relevant questions to ask yourself to be able to define the project delivery strategy, project delivery phasing, and organization maturity.

"Anyone can steer the ship, but it takes a leader to chart the course. Leaders who are good navigators are capable of taking their people just about anywhere." ~ John C. Maxwell

1. Project delivery strategy

What is the impact of the project, in other words:

- Is it a system development project?
- Is it a research project?
- Is it an implementation project?
- Is it an organizational development project?

What is the specificity of the project domain, in other words:

- Is it domain specific?
- Is it domain transcending but organization specific?
- Is it organization transcending (i.e. chain project)?

How can or should the project be delivered, in other words:

- Can or should the project be delivered in one go, the Big Bang scenario?
- Can the project be delivered in parts (per sub-system), and do these parts then stand alone, or do they depend on each other? That is of great importance for the phasing of the delivery.
- Are we dealing with a so-called evolutionary delivery? In this case, at the start of the project the result is not completely defined but depends on partial results that are gradually delivered, with each partial result leading to the next partial result and ultimately the final result.
- Is it a prototype project or pilot project to get an idea of the possible result?

Answering these questions will give you a pretty clear picture of the project, the results to deliver and the decision moments to continue with the project or not. That knowledge will give you directions for planning out your project execution.

2. Project execution phasing

Phasing the execution of the project greatly increases the chances of a successful project. Here are some tips:

- Keep maximum lead time within one year, preferably within nine months.
- Each partial delivery must yield a lasting result.
- Determine as many short-term milestones as possible, with the first milestone as soon as possible after the start of the project.

This way you can enforce success!

This kind of execution phasing also gives the feeling that things can still be stopped at any moment without much damage.

The objective here is to first win trust by increasing the chance of successful execution on a smaller scale.

Surefire Recipe for Planning Your Success

Plan your success by devising relatively small viable milestones. The premise is that each viable milestone should fit as, or be part of, a typical logical milestone. Viable means that it's feasible and has its own standalone purpose or value for your business goals.

The very first milestone you choose should be one you're sure will be achieved. This is essential, and it can surely be done if you put your creative mind to it. I know this works—I've successfully done and taught it for decades. If at first glance you don't have such a milestone, then devise one that fits the criteria as described. This way you start off with a surefire success.

Now, treat the next milestone as if it were a first milestone. In a sense, it really is your "next first" milestone. Remember success breeds success. By doing this you are stacking success upon success, finally resulting in a successful project.

Even if for some reason the project is abandoned before the deadline, you are still successful because you delivered viable milestones with value for your business goals. Practice this consistently and success will become second nature to you.

Note: This recipe was my contribution to the number-one Amazon bestselling book *Success is Yours!*

3. Organization maturity

You want to get an idea of the maturity of the organizations you are working with to determine how you can best deal with them. Where are possible bottlenecks to be expected? Identify the strengths and weaknesses.

I tend to say: "SWOT your organization before they sweat you out!"

You want to gain insight into the organizational structure you are working with.

- Is the organization organized in a strictly hierarchical manner, or is it more of a matrix organization?
- How are the responsibilities and accountabilities structured?
- Are there labor unions or any syndicates actively involved?
- What about the company's culture and flexibility? Open, willing and ready for change?
- Are there any other external influencing factors?

Not easy but necessary

I know, these are not easy questions to answer, but you should at least keep them in mind. It's all part of reading the environment to determine the best approach to deal with it.

1. Find the best delivery strategy and stick to it.
2. Use my Surefire Recipe as I mentioned above as best as possible in phasing your project execution. Following this recipe will set you apart from anyone else. Guaranteed!
3. SWOT the organizations you are working with and concentrate on the three most pressing complications that you find.

In the next chapter, I will dive deep into the balance of power between stakeholders.

Chapter 3.3: How to manage the power balance between stakeholders

What about the power balance between the stakeholders? Who should the leader approach to get something done? What is the best approach to reach them?

"If you can't influence people, then they will not follow you. And if people won't follow, you are not a leader. That's the Law of Influence."
~ John C. Maxwell

Dr. Martin Hetebrij, developer of the concept of communicative management about the workings of power and communication in organizations, has written a very enlightening and accessible book (sorry, but only available in the Dutch language) on the topic of power and politics in organizations.

Each leader has to cope with power. In this role, you must sometimes make decisions under time constraints, without a carefully conducted review in a democratic process of exchange of arguments. According to Hetebrij, that is exercising power. The use of power and the use of communication are tools of political acting. Political acting is, again according to Hetebrij, all acting that has to do with preparing, making and implementing decisions. Therefore, political acting is decision-oriented acting. In short, it's about influence and influencing.

In this context I will now explore the most important aspects of power and political acting.

- Reaching the right stakeholders to get the right things done right (*Force Field Analysis*)
- Balancing your power and trust position (*Strategic Triangle*)
- Managing your strategic position (*Strategic Political Acting*)
- Handling your own and others' power (*Practical Political Acting*)

1. Reaching the right stakeholders to get the right things done right

A *Force Field Analysis* is a very powerful and useful tool to draw a picture of the formal and informal balance of power within an organization.

First, you capture the formal balance of power in the form of a traditional organization chart. From your perspective as a leader, you position yourself in the center of the organization chart and then construct the rest of only the relevant stakeholders therearound.

Then you go in search of mutual personal relationships, or how people get along with each other. Are they "friend" or "foe" of each other? But how do you get that information? Firstly, by your perception from your own observations. Next by talking to people, and especially by listening to the stories in the corridors.

Here is an example of how this works.

Step 1: Formal power structure

Start by charting the formal organization structure and put yourself in the center of the chart. In this example you are Project Leader Y. Just chart the stakeholders that are relevant for your purpose of research at that moment. The result is the formal power structure illustrating the different obvious power centers that are mostly top-down oriented. Such a power center is, for instance, Project Leader Y and Team 1 through Team 4.

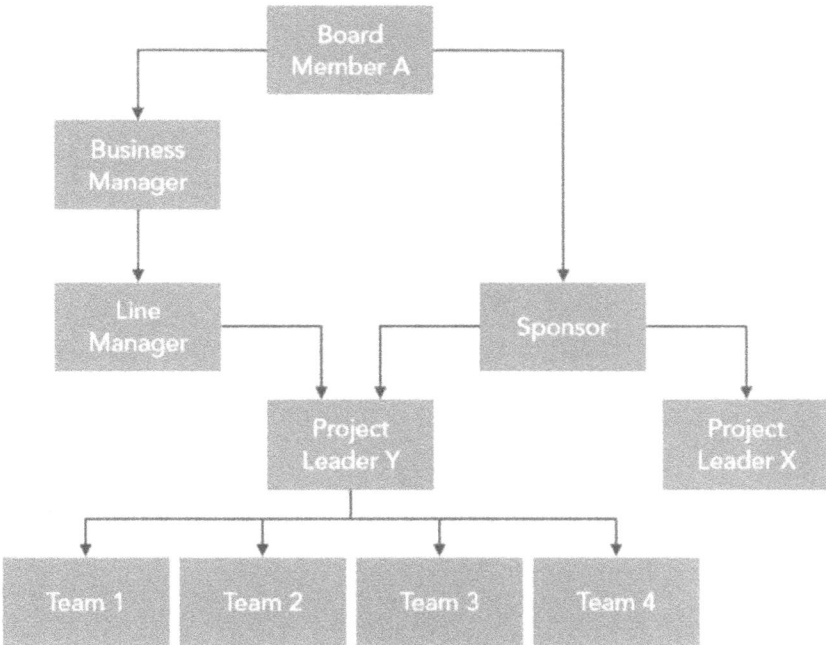

Step 2: Friend relationships

Research who is "friend" with whom, no matter their formal relationships. Draw solid green arrows to make this visible in your formal power structure. In this example, the nodes N1 through N5 represent the informal power centers. So N1 indicates that the Business Manager, the Line Manager, and the Project Leader Y have a friendly relationship outside their hierarchical relationship.

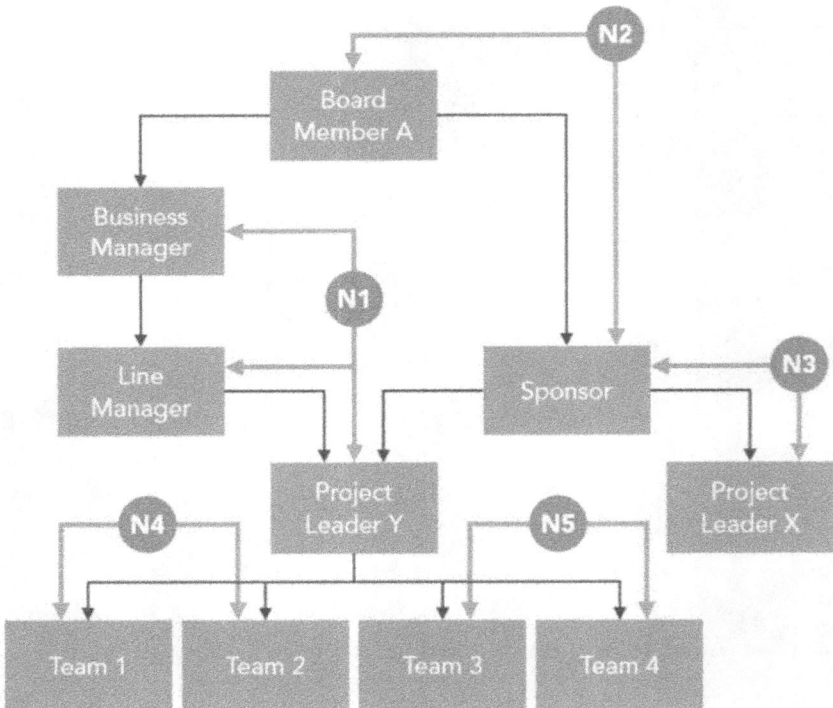

Step 3: Foe relationships

This time you research who is "foe" with whom, no matter their formal relationships. Draw red dotted lines to make this visible in your formal power structure. There are no new power centers here; after all, we are charting "foe" relationships. In my example, the Board Member A has a "foe" relation with the Business Manager. That also goes for the Line Manager and the Sponsor.

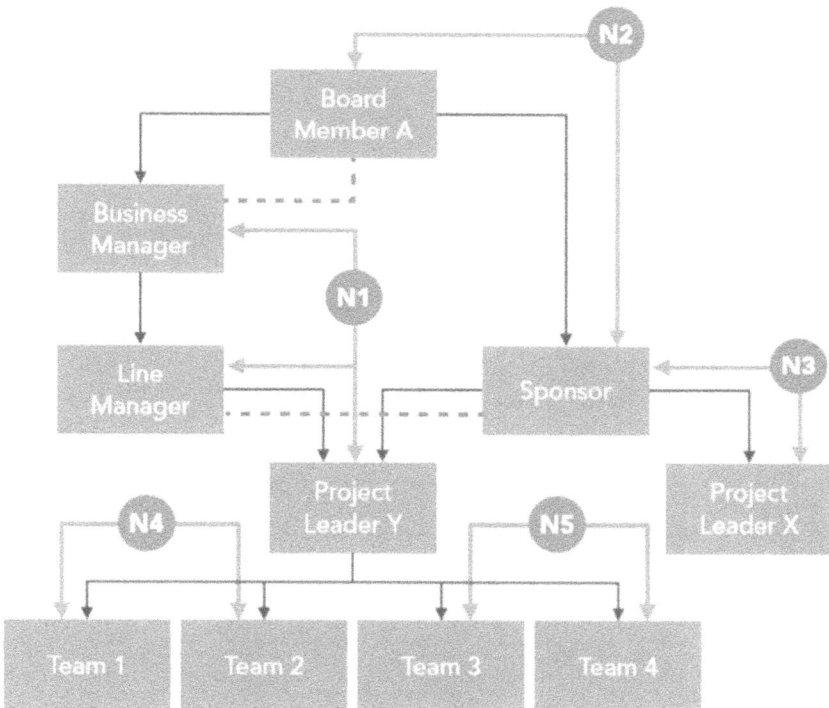

Step 4: Power centers at work

Now you have a picture of the formal and informal power balance related to your purpose of research. With this information you can seek out the best ways to reach the stakeholders you want to do business with. Either you want to approach them directly or through a "friend" relation. But remember this is a snapshot—relationships do change along the way.

Now let's look at some example cases to illustrate the use of the Force Field Analysis.

First case

You want to gain access to someone with whom you have no direct formal or informal relationship.

Look at the informal centers of power you are part of to see if someone within those groups has access to that person. It's even better if these two individuals themselves are together in an informal power center. Then let this person provide you access to your desired person. If this fails, then you know that you yourself have to establish a relationship with the person you want to access.

Second case

You have formal access to a particular person but it's not working between you two.

In this case, you should find someone in your informal power centers who can get along well with that person and put him or her at work to improve your relationship with that person.

Third case

There are two people outside your formal and informal influence who are important for your project, but these two people can't get along with each other.

Here again, search for someone in your informal centers of power who can get along with both people and put him or her at work to achieve your goal.

Fourth case

Your informal power position as Project Leader Y in the example case needs some balancing on the Sponsor side.

You have a friendly informal power position on the Line Manager side, while the Line Manager has a hostile power position with the Sponsor. You only seem to have a formal relationship with the Sponsor. It might be quite beneficial for you to establish a friendly relationship with the Sponsor. That will provide you with a power position in the center of the whole power structure.

You will encounter many situations where you can make good use of a Force Field Analysis. After you have done this a few times, you don't even have to map it out anymore. You can do it in your head in a flash. Again, remember that such an analysis is a snapshot, so it is important to perform this exercise regularly to keep up with the relationships within the organization. Best practice is to perform a Force Field Analysis at the very moment you need its results.

2. Balancing your power and trust position

To perform your role successfully and live up to your responsibility, your power position and your position of trust should be well balanced. This is also called the *Strategic Triangle*. This balance is determined by the extent to which your power position and your position of trust enable you to work properly.

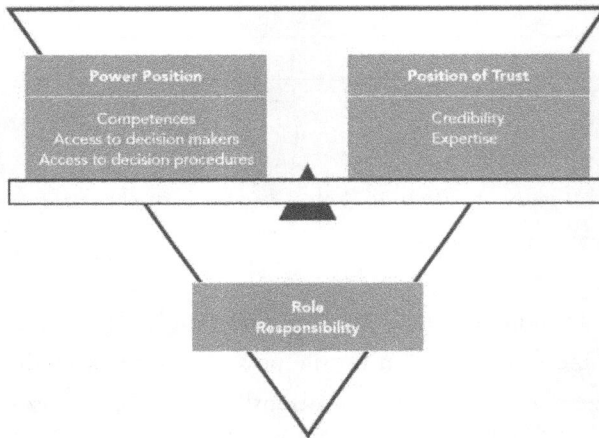

Power Position
Competences
Access to decision makers
Access to decision procedures

Position of Trust
Credibility
Expertise

Role
Responsibility

Your power position is characterized by your competencies, your access to decision makers and your access to decision-making procedures. Your position of trust is characterized by your credibility and your expertise.

Normally you are recruited as a (project) leader, by one or more decision makers, based on your perceived expertise. Also, you receive some privileges and access to certain decision-making procedures.

At the start, you rely on your alleged expertise that you have yet to prove. Upon proving your expertise, your credibility will also increase. With that, when desired, you can easily obtain more competences or access to more decision makers and decision-making procedures, or both.

Pay sufficient attention to the characteristics of both positions. The more balanced they are, the more successful you will be.

Remember, as a leader you are in a strategic position. The strategic importance of that placement is determined by those parties with whom you want to maintain or strengthen your position to avoid any conflicts.

3. Managing your strategic position

This part, also known as *Strategic Political Acting*, is aimed at your strategic position as a leader. It's about obtaining, restoring, preserving, and extending your strategic position.

You do this through the characteristics of your power position and your position of trust in your Strategic Triangle. Your basic skills as a pragmatic leader, as covered in the Grit Pillar, will come in handy here. That also goes for the use of the Force Field Analysis.

Use your Strategic Triangle and the Force Field Analysis to manage your strategic position.

4. Handling your own and others' power

Practical Political Acting is focused on handling power. By power, I mean power according to Hetebrij, as an instrument of political acting.

Using your own power
In organizations or teams, the use of power mainly comes down to taking charge. The person who is in charge has the power to impose decisions, give assignments, set goals, and assess employees or team members on their results.

Responding to the power of others
Responding to power is an active act of rejecting or obeying. Answering power in organizations is the same as receiving guidance. Anyone who receives guidance actively thinks, gives feedback, or opposes, or pretends to obey and undermines the manager's or leader's position. Responding to power has a major impact on the quality of management.

Delegating power to others
You can pass (some of) your power to others. Delegating power means assigning positions to people. In organizations we distinguish positions to which we assign responsibilities and people.

Mobilizing the power of others
If you have no power yourself, you can use the power of another. As a leader you normally have enough power to do your job. Sometimes it can be necessary or even handy to utilize the power of someone else to achieve your goals. One of the ways to do that is to make that person co-responsible for the results.

"Know what is happening around you. Be in control of what is happening within you." ~ Bob Proctor

Handling power is certainly a core activity of a leader to get things done!

Again, your basic skills as a pragmatic leader, as covered in the Grit Pillar, will come in handy here.

At this point, you've made it through the main content of the Grip Pillar. What follows is some action taking, bonus material, and a case study. Just because I didn't denominate them as main content doesn't mean they are not important. They reinforce the main content. So take some time and go through them. The case study is a typical illustration of how making key players co-responsible can make the difference between success and failure.

Your Grip Call-for-Action:
Do a Force Field Analysis

➔ Know how to successfully reach your stakeholders. ⬅

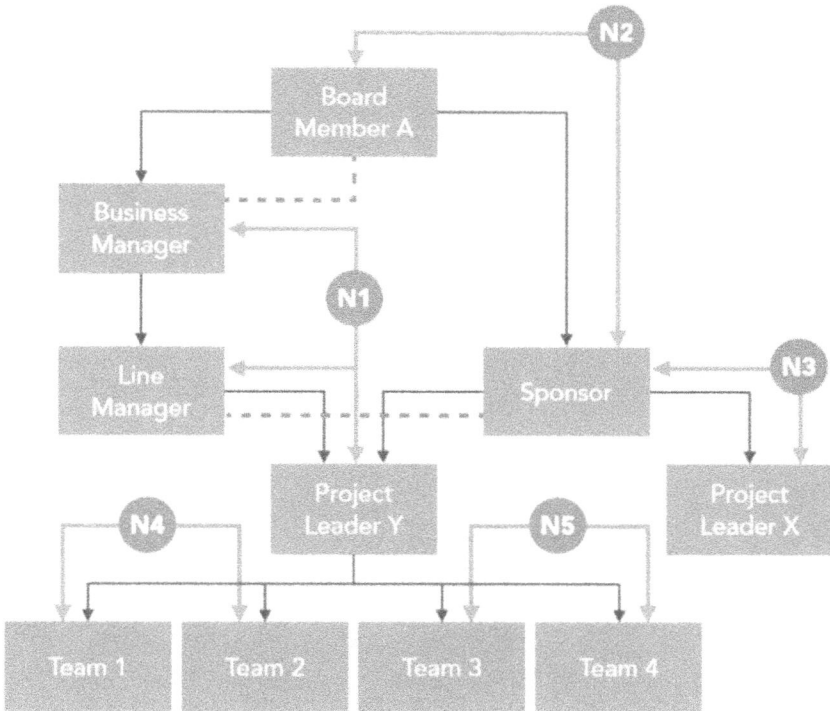

Your Grip Call-for-Reflection: Are You in Control?

Are you ready for change and growth, aka "Knoster proof"?

Do you know the profile of your operating environment?

Are your power position and position of trust well balanced?

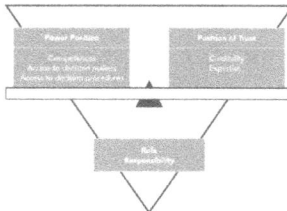

Bonus Chapter 1: Fast-track tool to determine personality types

Working with teams is working with people with different personalities. Knowing their personality type and corresponding characteristics will give you an edge on how to best approach them. This is especially true when it comes to power and politics.

There are many methods and tools out there to help you do this. Here is a fast-track tool to determine personality types by approximation. You can also use it to determine your own personality type.

This fast-track tool is derived from the 16 Myers-Briggs Type Indicator (MBTI), which is based on Carl Jung's theory of psychological type. It indicates personality preferences in four dimensions:

Focusing Attention	E = Extraversion, the outer world or I = Introversion, the inner world
Processing Information	S = Sensing, factual decisions or N = INtuition, gut decisions

Making Decisions	T = Thinking, logical and analytic or F = Feeling, different perspectives
Dealing with the world	J = Judging, rules and routines or P = Perceiving, spontaneous and impulsive

The four letters that represent someone's personality type can help them understand themselves and their interactions with others.

This fast-track tool gives you the opportunity to determine your stakeholders' and team members' four letters by approximation, and with that their personality type. Close enough to know how to approach them best.

1. Determine the "Letter"

- For each of the four dimensions there is a column with some typical characteristics per personality preferences (the "Letter").
- Use the knowledge you have about the person to choose which letter fits best or most of the time according to the corresponding characteristics.
- Note the four determined letters.

Focusing Attention

E = Extraversion	I = Introversion
• Gets energy from being around people. • Needs to talk to other people to figure out solutions. • Motivated by people. • Needs alone time but gets drained if not around people enough.	• Gets energy from being alone. • Needs to think things through alone. • Motivated by inner world. • People drain them.

Processing Information

S = Sensing	N = Intuition
• Usually traditional, trust establishment, rules and regulations. • Gathers a lot of facts, details, and data about a person or subject matter. • Makes calculated judgments.	• Able to see the big picture, theory, and long-term. • Brainstorms a lot. • Tends to have sudden, strong judgments, gut feeling.

Making Decisions

T = Thinking	F = Feeling
• Uses logic to make choices. • Often black and white, not much gray area. • Rational thinking.	• Sees different perspectives before making decisions. • Considers others' feelings when making decisions. • Compassionate.

Dealing with the World

J = Judging	P = Perceiving
• Enjoys routines and to-do lists. • Scheduled. • Organized. • Structure.	• Tends to be spontaneous. • Go with the flow and flexible. • Enjoy surprises and changing plans.

By approximation you have determined a combination of four letters representing one of the 16 different personality types.

2. Determine Personality Type

Take the four determined letters and use the table to find the corresponding personality type. Let me emphasize that the illustrated characteristics per personality type are not extensive. I only show those characteristics that are useful to you as a leader to decide how to approach your stakeholders and team members.

Table Personality Types Based upon original work by Victor Gulenko and modified for the purpose of this book	
ENTP (The Inventor)	**ISFP (The Peacemaker)**
• ability to mobilize in extreme conditions • counterattacks when under pressure • likes to give advice proposing radical solutions • works fast but quality suffers	• productive when working for themselves • doesn't like to criticize people openly • doesn't get involved in confrontations • always tries to keep away from authoritative figures

• chaotic but generates reform from destruction • often becomes leader	• doesn't like briefings and other boring business meetings • negotiates on an informal level • maintains peaceful relations with everyone
ESFJ (The Enthusiast) • keeps asking if has been understood • easily makes new friends • motivated by pure enthusiasm • sharp wit in business matters • difficulties judging when enough is enough • appreciates help with home matters • getting help is more important than the result	**INTJ (The Analyst)** • never shows initiative first and maintains psychological distance • very clear and logical • maintains self-control • not inclined to talk about their private life • combines the need for freedom with a feeling of responsibility • ignores rules, concepts and directives • not understood and mostly avoided
ENFJ (The Actor) • enjoys the company of positive people • possesses the ability to be a great orator • likes to fantasize • tendency to create problems where there aren't • respects hierarchy, disrespectful to those lower in position • doesn't like to work under observation • has no problems undertaking difficult tasks	**ISTJ (The Pragmatist)** • easily interacts with strangers • pays great attention to facts and figures • very realistic • always ready to share knowledge with others • adapts well to positions of power and is very dutiful • likes to collect reference material • reads manuals before using new appliances

ESTP (The Conqueror)	INFP (The Romantic)
• always shows positive emotions • pays full attention during interactions • gains people's trust very quickly • likes to explain things to others • focuses on the opponent's weaknesses • doesn't care much how people achieve results • prefers to adopt informal and unofficial leadership	• often delays the inevitable until the last moment • always finds excuses to justify lack of responsibility • has a good instinct for commercial and business matters • maintains a firm grip on positions of power • has the ability to positively console people in trouble • has very flexible, consciously controlled emotions • appreciates people who show concern for their problems
ESFP (The Ambassador)	INTP (The Observer)
• reacts with hostility to rules, limits or discipline • openly demonstrates real feelings toward others • likes to provoke positive emotions in others • knows well how to manipulate people's feelings • often has a wide circle of acquaintances • looks for immediate returns in projects • constantly look for challenges	• can be very pushy when interacting with others • is good at noticing contradictions in theories or opinions • can predict people's next moves • is very skeptical about new beginnings • has good abilities to calculate profit quickly • isn't afraid to run big businesses • pays a lot of attention to details

ENTJ (The Pioneer)	ISFJ (The Guardian)
• likes to joke and play tricks on others	• analyzes situations logically and objectively
• finds it very easy to start conversations	• has a very well-developed sense of duty
• is open to new proposals, but investigates the practicality	• replies effectively to people with sharp tongues
• quickly realizes the potential of new ideas	• feels uncomfortable alone with a person for a long time
• is quite responsible and likes to be in command	• doesn't cope well with indefinite situations
• works hard and quickly and likes to experiment	• doesn't like to wait for impending events
• can be careless	• likes orderliness and cleanliness
ESTJ (The Director)	**INFJ (The Empath)**
• always polite when interacting with strangers	• can be very touchy and this may strain a conversation
• likes to ask questions and find out facts	• has a special ability to listen to people
• a great supporter of practicality	• cares not with words but with real actions
• doesn't like sudden changes	• has the reputation of being naive and impractical
• has a tremendous ability to work	• does everything carefully, paying attention to quality
• often displays the qualities of a good organizer	• knows how to establish peace between conflicting sides
• has a straightforward approach to goals	• doesn't like to stand out
ENFP (The Reporter)	**ISTP (The Artisan)**
• knows how to find that special way of dealing with people	• skeptical in evaluations and stubborn in opinions

• helps people extricate themselves from difficult situations • is often optimistic and that usually rubs off on others • pays the least attention possible to details • has a characteristic ability to create a circle of friends • is quick to get mobilized in extreme situations • strives for improvisation and unplanned actions	• barely shares feelings with others • tries to extract a practical use from everything • not powered only by enthusiasm • demands complete independence • usually follows own convictions • has a great deal of persistence

Bonus Chapter 2: How to qualify your stakeholders

At the start of any project, you want to know who your stakeholders are and identify their interests and influence. Yes, you can make a list of all the stakeholders with their distinctive features and go from there. Here's another approach that I find very helpful.

Be aware of three paramount aspects of stakeholders.

1. Who are the direct stakeholders and who are the indirect stakeholders?
2. What is the stakeholder impact on the project and vice versa?
3. How do stakeholders influence the main sponsor?

This knowledge will help you determine your level of engagement with your stakeholders. It can also help you to decide how to get engaged with your stakeholders and through whom (influencer) if necessary.

1. Direct and Indirect Stakeholders

Direct stakeholders are the ones who are directly connected to the organization (or even a department of this organization) that immediately benefits from the results of the project. That's mostly where the main sponsor and key players come from.

Indirect stakeholders are the ones who have an interest outside of the organization, e.g. suppliers, contractors, consultants, and even other departments of the main organization, etc.

This information is useful if you want insight into the goals of the different stakeholders. That can help you respond adequately to possible conflicting goals.

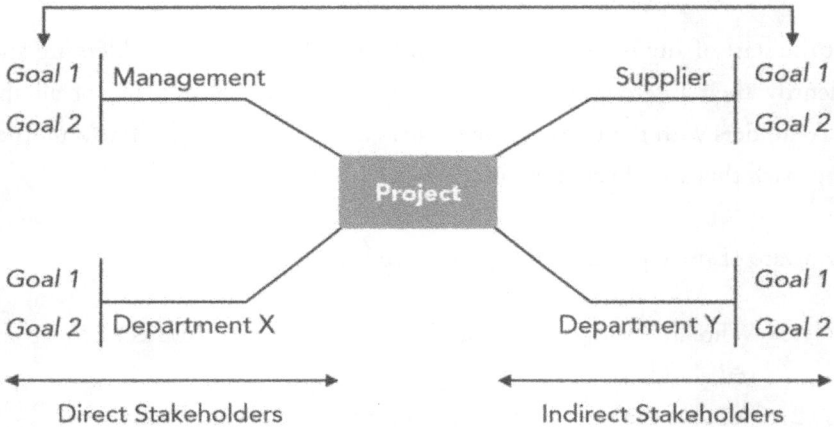

You map out the stakeholders in a mind map fashion, putting the project in the center. On one side of the map, let's say the left side, you draw a line for each direct stakeholder. You do the same on the other side, the right side, for the indirect stakeholders. For each stakeholder you note their main goals. And you draw arrows between stakeholders that have a mutual relationship.

2. Stakeholder Impact versus Project Impact

It's obvious that stakeholders have an impact on the project one way or the other. It's also a fact that the results of the project can have an impact on the stakeholders.

This information is useful if you want to know which stakeholder has the greatest impact or decision-making power or both, and how important the stakeholders are relative to each other.

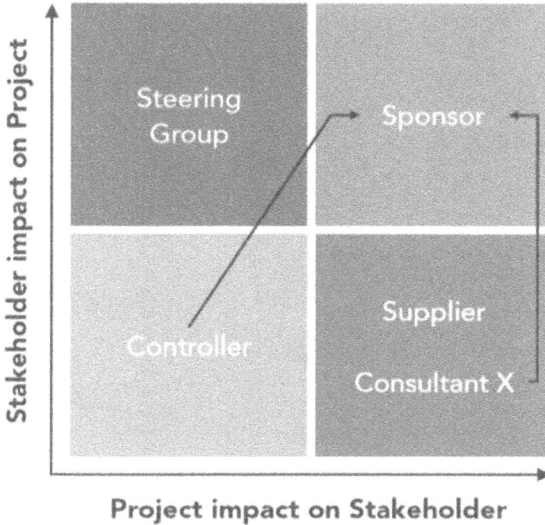

Draw a square with the x-axis being the "Project Impact on Stakeholder," and the y-axis being the "Stakeholder Impact on Project." Divide the square into four quadrants. Place each stakeholder in a quadrant based on their impact on the project and the impact of the project on them. The most important stakeholder will fit in the upper right quadrant. And you draw arrows between stakeholders that have a mutual relationship.

3. Stakeholder Influence on Sponsor

This information is useful if you want to clarify the mutual relationships between the stakeholders and their role in the project.

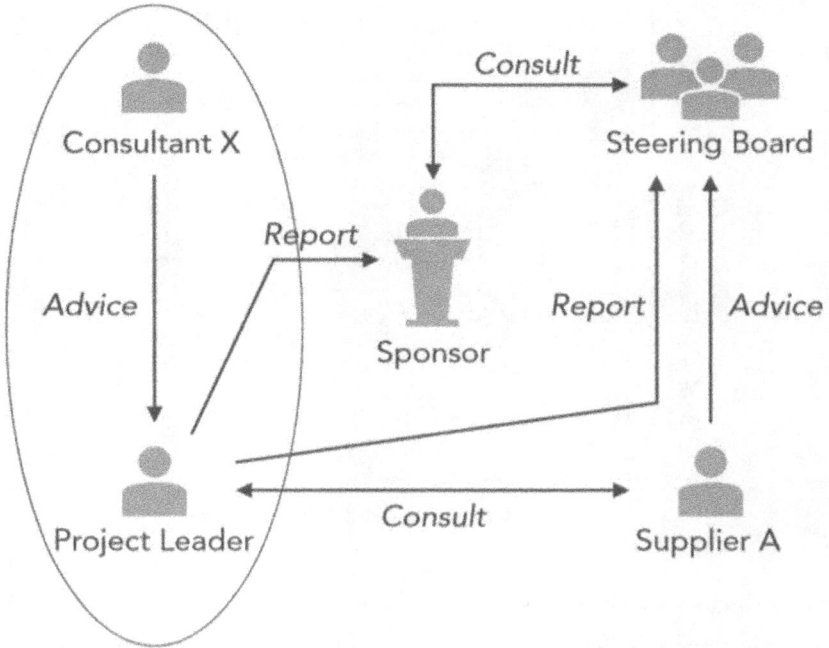

Draw the most important stakeholder (the sponsor, the decision maker) in the middle of your sheet. Then draw the most important influencing stakeholders around the sponsor. Connect them with arrows and note the mutual relations. Now add the less important influencers, possibly using a different color. Again, you add arrows for the mutual relations and labels for the characteristics of the relationship. You can also draw circles around the influencers that belong together, for example because they work at the same organization or department.

Case Study: How making key players co-responsible turned a hostile organization merger into a success

The Client

Department of defense with multiple independent telematics management organizations to support and maintain dozens of technical domains and hundreds of applications. These assets are crucial for smooth and dependable military and civic operations, nationally and internationally. The staff consists of a mix of military and civilian personnel.

The Challenge

Political leadership and military command decided to cut costs and implement more efficiency by merging the existing telematics management organizations into less independently operating organizations. They're starting with the regional merging of three important directorates situated in the northwestern part of the country with the national command garrison.

The goal is not only to merge the four separate management organizations, but also to introduce an ITIL-based and process-oriented working method and corporate culture. All to be done in a politically sensitive environment in which the individual management organizations are hostile to the merge.

Although all personnel knew that the decision to merge was irreversible, they still mobilized all available forces to postpone the implementation to get better personal conditions. Especially the civilian personnel were not eager to move to another city or maybe even become obsolete. The military personnel had no choice other than to go along. Next to that, many civilians were looking forward to their soon retirement and had no desire to move with their families.

Military command was responsible for this reorganization and decided to hire an independent external project manager to lead the merge process. In their selection procedure, they selected me due to my experience in IT and communication projects with organizational components.

My assignment was to realize the merge of the technical facilities, implement the ITIL-based and process-oriented working method as a starting point for the new corporate culture, and last but not least secure the cooperation of the personnel. All of that without causing any political turmoil. I got 18 months to get the job done. I had to report directly to the military command general, who was my formal project sponsor.

My Solution

I had enough experience with similar IT and reorganizational projects. So I had no concerns about the technical merge and the implementation of the ITIL-based and process-oriented working method. I could hire additional professionals to help out in the implementation phase if necessary. After all, I was chosen because of my experience and professional contacts.

The whole project would fail or succeed depending on the cooperation and collaboration of the personnel. I had to come up with a plan or approach to secure cooperation. The more take-it-or-leave-it military approach wouldn't cut it with the civilian personnel. I had to find a win-win solution.

I decided to plan a plenary meeting with all the personnel involved with the merge where I would unfold my plan for the technical merge and the implementation of the ITIL-based and process-oriented working method. After my presentation I would take the time for Q&A. My reason for this plenary meeting was to get an opportunity to "read the room" with everyone present. I wanted to discover the natural leaders in the room and those people with outspoken opinions who also had a following. I was especially interested in the opponents of the reorganization. I was looking for my key players!

I held the meeting in the auditorium of the main building where about 90 percent of the personnel showed up. That would be over a hundred people. After my presentation I answered all their questions and concerns, but I also asked them how they would cope with the issues the audience addressed. In the meantime I found my key players. They came out of all levels of the workforce. And I got some very useful ideas to work with.

Over the next few days I gathered some information about the key players I had in mind. I did that by file research and also by interviewing people near to my potential key players. Then I had a one-on-one talk with each of them and explained to them that I was looking for key players to participate on my advisory board.

This advisory board would address all merge issues including typical personnel issues of a general nature. The goal was to advise a solution to each presented issue or concern. Where necessary I would consult with my sponsor. Once we decided on a solution and had the green light from command, we would each defend and "sell" the solution to the respective followings.

All the key players agreed to work with me this way. In practice we quite easily worked through the technical and organizational issues and concerns. Some personnel issues were more challenging than others, and occasionally I had to work out a solution with the human resource department.

The lesson of this case is that no matter how hostile your environment is, read your stakeholders and find a way to get them on board to work with you productively. Make them feel that they matter and can contribute to success for the organization and themselves. Give them trust and co-responsibility.

My key players became my most reliable advocates and helped me deliver a successful project within the given timeframe.

The Results

The desired merge of the technical facilities and the implementation of the ITIL-based and process-oriented working method were delivered fully operational in the given timeframe within 18 months.

The cooperation of the personnel was secured with a win-win approach where they took their responsibility.

Individual workers were able to negotiate an acceptable solution for their concerns.

There was no political turmoil. That was a great relief for the political leadership and military command.

I got a nice farewell party with a buffet, a nice bottle of wine, and a special recommendation from my sponsor, the military command general. We were both very satisfied with the results of our efforts to make this merger a success.

You, your stakeholders, and your environment are set to go! Anything else?

Yes, at this point you've got all the necessary parameters in place for success. Your mindset is focused on success, your stakeholders are eager to follow your lead, and you've got the operating environment under control.

But what if I set you up with some specific tools to help you get there easier and faster? Then go for your last step, the Gear Pillar to help you create the conditions to set the tone. Get "Gear" and prepare to secure your leadership!

Pillar #4: Gear

"Create the conditions to set the tone."

In the previous three pillars, you learned how to set yourself, your stakeholders, and your environment up for success. That's the primary goal of this book. Having a few specific tools at your disposal will help you get there easier and faster. That's what this pillar is about—specific tools to create the conditions to set the tone. Harness these tools to enforce your leadership!

Chapter 4.0: Harness the right tools to enforce your leadership with ease

This pillar concerns what I call the rational core aspect of pragmatic leadership where I propose some useful leadership tools. It's all about the leader's gear to set the conditions for a successful endeavor.

There are many management methods and approaches out there. As you know by now, this book is about leadership, not about management in the traditional sense. Of course, there are some management tools that a leader will use, and they should, but those don't fall within the scope of this book.

I will address a few basic tools that I believe are very useful for a pragmatic leader to set the right conditions, to set the tone. They will help you secure the collaboration (the 2 Cs) of all your stakeholders.

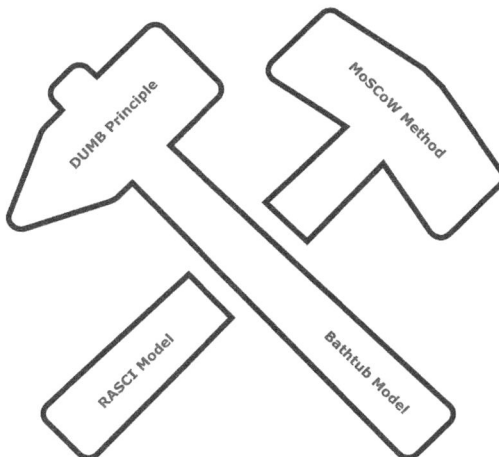

The presented tools are focused on the more relational aspects of leadership, the people you deal with. Because that's where the magic has to take place. There is where you lay your practical foundation for your daily success.

With these tools you will be able to:

- Define your vision
- Set priorities
- Set up communication lines
- Explain your level of engagement
- Secure collaboration of stakeholders

As I said earlier, these are your basic tools. In my opinion this means you need all of them to set the conditions to obtain enough control. Then you and your stakeholders will know what to expect of each other. There is mutual consensus and the boundaries and responsibilities are clear.

Combine these tools with your other preferred management tools and you're ready to go. Now your leadership toolbox contains the necessary conditioning and measuring tools. All you have to do is use them wisely.

Let me deliberate a little on the use of tools in general. Tools can be a blessing or a curse depending on how you use them. Use them with integrity for their original purpose. Use them to give you insight, not to merely make a point that serves you conveniently. This is especially the case with tools that provide numerical data.

Traditional management tools are often numerical data driven and therefore more objective, but nevertheless easily subject to manipulative interpretation. The tools I describe in this book are more of a procedural and subjective nature. Here the interpretation is a matter of the degree of complying with the mutually agreed upon values, actions, and responsibilities.

The point I want to make here is to choose and use your tools carefully, wisely and with integrity. And less is more when it comes to the set of useful tools in your toolbox. I've often seen the misuse of tools that always leads to wrong decisions in the long run. Not to mention unrepairable complications in carefully built relationships.

The next chapter describes a tool to define your vision without being distracted.

Chapter 4.1: How to think DUMB before you plan SMART

As a leader, you translate your vision into goals and tasks that are defined as S.M.A.R.T.—specific, measurable, attainable, realistic, time-bound—to make them manageable. But if you submit your vision to the S.M.A.R.T. principle, you will stifle your creativity to think outside of the box. Brendon Burchard, number-one *New York Times* bestselling author and founder of High-Performance Academy, came up with the D.U.M.B. principle to help you get your inspiration to flow freely with drive and grit.

Bring forth a desire that is unbounded and even scares you a little bit, that will demand all the best that is in you, that takes you out of your comfort zone to achieve the remarkable. That kind of desire provides you with visions that make you stand out to offer a meaningful contribution.

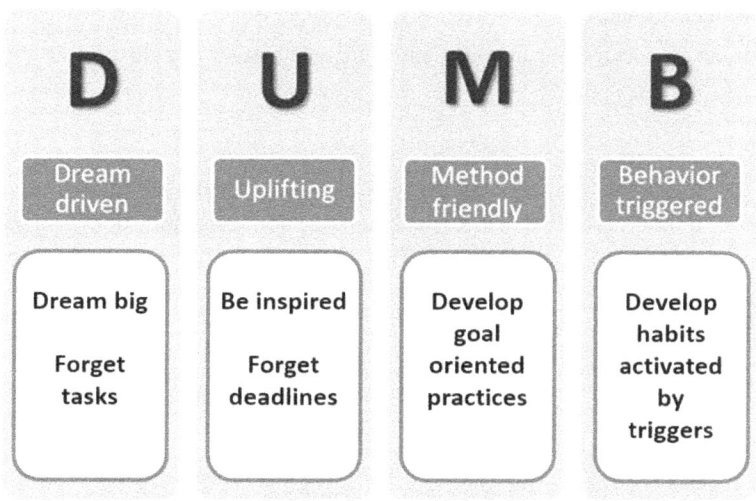

D	U	M	B
Dream driven	Uplifting	Method friendly	Behavior triggered
Dream big Forget tasks	Be inspired Forget deadlines	Develop goal oriented practices	Develop habits activated by triggers

Dream-driven
Dream big, think out of the box. Set your goals in alignment with your bigger vision.

Uplifting
Set inspiring, positive, joyous, uplifting goals for yourself.

Method-friendly
Set goals that allow for creating methods and practices that help you to achieve them. That's how you distinguish a goal from a task.

Behavior triggered
Create a behavioral trigger that reminds you to chase your goal.

The D.U.M.B. bottom line is to first go for the WHAT from within your WHY. Don't be distracted by the HOW and the WHEN. S.M.A.R.T. will take care of the HOW and the WHEN.
Using this principle can help you find your ultimate vision. Now go out there, dream big and come up with a vision that makes a difference. Remember that S.M.A.R.T. planning comes after D.U.M.B. visioning.

Nobody can explain the D.U.M.B. principle better than Brendon Burchard himself, so I encourage you to see his vivid explanation in this video: https://bit.ly/2X3zKdI

The next chapter explores a tool to prioritize requirements in collaboration with your stakeholders.

Chapter 4.2: How to prioritize requirements in a collaborative fashion

As a leader in your quest for change and growth, you have requirements to meet. Requirements need to be prioritized because stakeholders can't always have everything they want, or rather because we can't always give them everything they want. That is not because we don't want to, but because most projects are faced with a limited budget and time frame.

The MoSCoW technique is used to prioritize requirements collaboratively. That means you use this tool together with your (important) stakeholders. Using this method for prioritization can help you secure collaboration (the 2 Cs) of all stakeholders doing the right things in the agreed order.

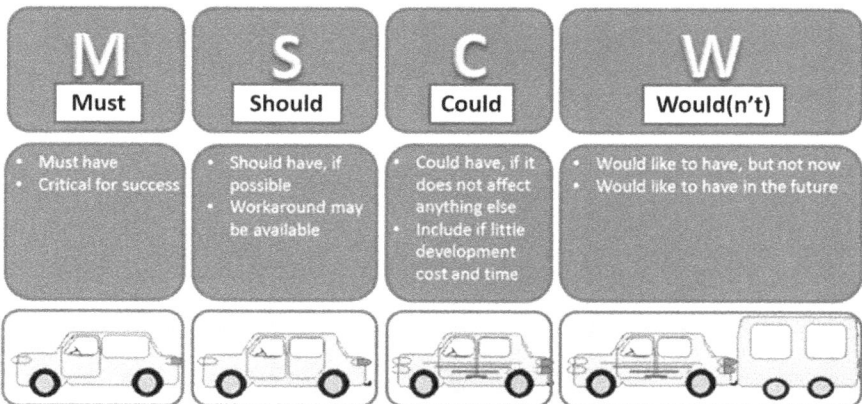

It's not necessary to go deeper into the workings of the MoSCoW technique here. I'm sure most leaders, if not all leaders, have heard of or are familiar with this technique. If not, you can find out all about it on the internet. As they say, google it. But more importantly, use it to prioritize requirements!

See this short video where the Agile Academy explains the MoSCoW method in a practical situation:
https://bit.ly/2k8iDlD

The next chapter refers to a tool to set up effective communication lines with your stakeholders.

Chapter 4.3: How to communicate effectively with each level of your stakeholders

As a leader, you are confronted with different types of stakeholders that all contribute to your objectives on a different level. The RASCI model helps you determine the most effective way of communicating with each level of contribution.

First identify what the tasks are, who is responsible for each task, who will support each task, those you need to consult and finally those who need to be informed to keep the communication channels open. By making the model clear, everyone knows what is expected.

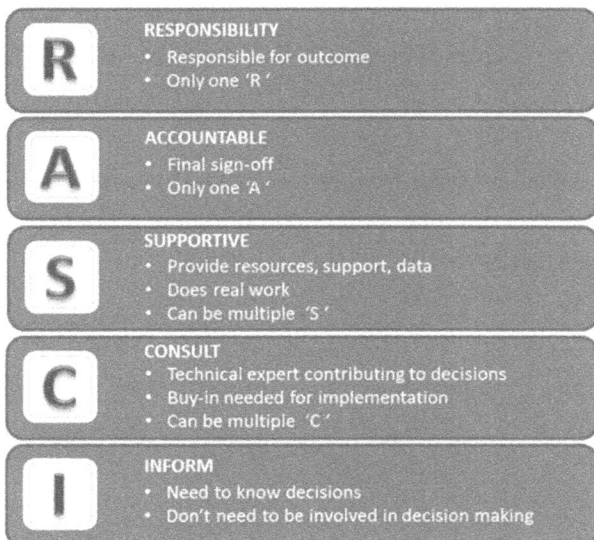

R — **RESPONSIBILITY**
- Responsible for outcome
- Only one 'R'

A — **ACCOUNTABLE**
- Final sign-off
- Only one 'A'

S — **SUPPORTIVE**
- Provide resources, support, data
- Does real work
- Can be multiple 'S'

C — **CONSULT**
- Technical expert contributing to decisions
- Buy-in needed for implementation
- Can be multiple 'C'

I — **INFORM**
- Need to know decisions
- Don't need to be involved in decision making

A few points to consider when setting up your RASCI:

- Each task can only have one "A"—too many chiefs never works.
- You can't have a task without an "A"—you won't get any traction if nobody owns the task.
- There should only be one "R." If you have too many, you'll hinder the speed at which you can execute the task.
- You need to have at least one "C" and "I" to ensure that the wider audience is aware of what is happening, and that you keep the communication channels open.

Ensure all involved provide feedback, approve and are collaborating to help you get the best result possible. The RASCI model helps the team to get the important stuff done. Use this model to break down your tasks, goals, and projects into achievable chunks and go forth to meet your objectives.

Using this model for effective communication can help you secure collaboration (the 2 Cs) where all stakeholders know what is expected of them.

It's not necessary to go deeper into the workings of the RASCI model here. I'm sure most leaders, if not all leaders, have heard of or are familiar with this technique. If not, you can find out all about it on the internet. Again, google it.

See this short video by David Mathew (Teams and Leadership) on how to use RASCI to agree on team roles and responsibilities in a practical situation: https://bit.ly/31sz7K8

The next chapter introduces a tool to explain your level of engagement with your stakeholders.

Chapter 4.4: How to explain your level of engagement

Ed Muzio, CEO of Group Harmonics and author of *Make Work Great,* defined the Bathtub Model for leaders to engage with their teams and explain that their level of engagement will vary over time. It is important for leaders to be overt and clear with their staffs as to their level of engagement in advance, so that lack of contribution is not misconstrued as management detachment or ineffective leadership. The Bathtub Model allows leaders and managers to express trust in their teams while still retaining the right to involve themselves in critical components of the work.

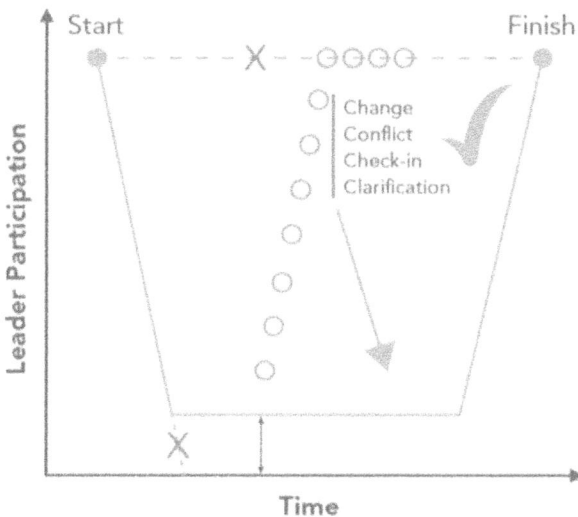

The Bathtub Model is not (yet) widely enough known, and that's a pity because it's a very useful tool for leaders. That's why I'll go through the four stages here in more depth.

Stage 1: Highly involved

On the vertical axis, we have the leader's participation; this is how much you interact with your team. On the horizontal axis, we have time; this could be in days, weeks or months depending on how long the project will go on.

Early in the project [Start], you have a high level of participation; here you are high on the axis, putting the team together, defining the scope, etc.

Fast forward to the end [Finish] where the project comes to conclusion, the team got their result and you are rewarding and recognizing them, and again as the leader, you have a high level of involvement.

But it would be a mistake to assume that your involvement level will stay high throughout the life of the project.

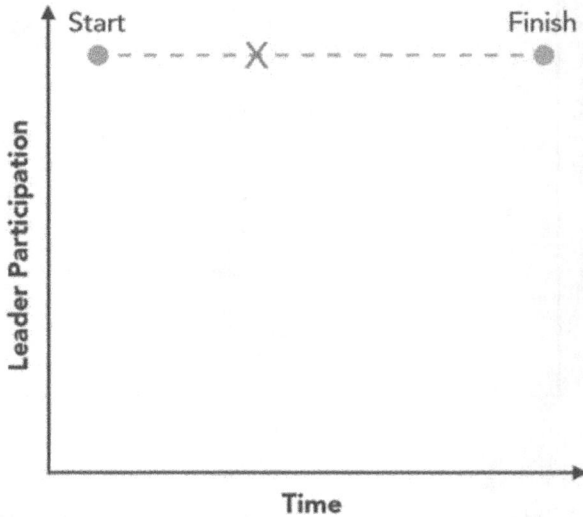

Stage 2: Somewhat involved

As the leader your participation will come down and stay at a low level for much of the project and then come back up at the end, forming the bathtub shape.

That is a way of telling your team that after the start of the project, you are going to get out their way and allow them to use their expertise to do their work. You are not going to micromanage them.

But you are not going to go all the way to zero. You are going to be somewhat involved, somewhat engaged.

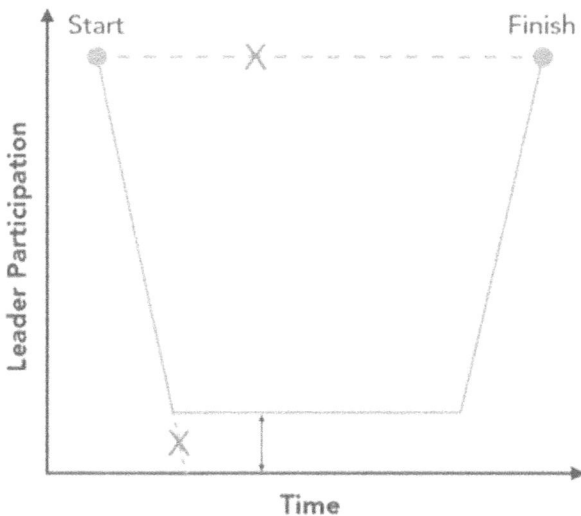

Stage 3: Slightly involved unless

Here is why the analogy works so well. You can say as the leader you are going to have a low level of engagement for much of the time, but if certain things come up you are going to get more engaged.

For instance, if there's a change in scope or direction, if there's a conflict within the team or between teams, if there's a check-in point that we agreed on for primary review of the status, or where there's a clarification needed to get the work done, you will then bubble up and get a lot more involved.

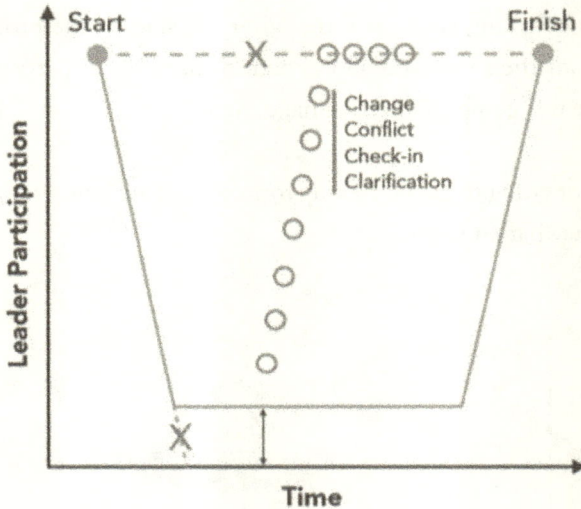

Stage 4: Highly involved until

You will be highly involved for a little while dealing with these issues and after the issues are over, you will drop back down the bottom in the tub, get out of the way again and let your team do their work.

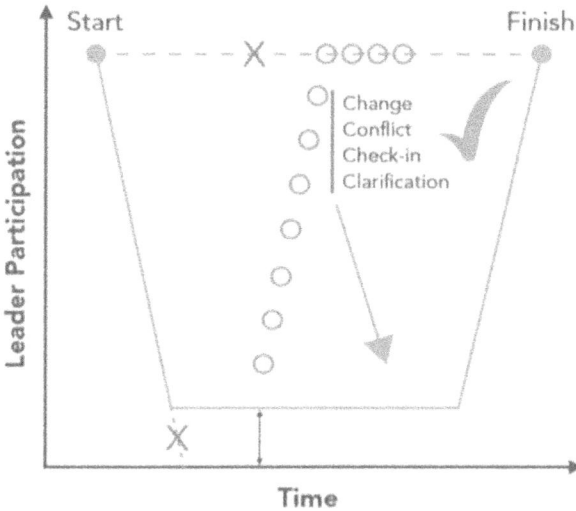

The Benefits

Drawing this model has a couple of benefits. First of all, you're letting the team know what to anticipate before you back away. That way they don't think you are making an excuse. You are explaining they should expect you to come down the slope.

Next, it reminds you as a leader that you need to be watchful, paying attention for changes, conflicts, check-ins, and clarifications needed, so that you know when it's time to bubble back up and get involved.

So, the next time you are leading or sponsoring a project, at the very beginning before anything starts, take a few minutes to sketch out the Bathtub Model. Let your team know what to expect. They will appreciate not being micromanaged. They will know what to expect from you and they will know when to come to you with an issue. Because then you are going to bubble up and help them.

Using this model for efficient communication can help you secure collaboration (the 2 Cs) where your team knows what is expected of them and when to actively involve you in a higher degree of engagement.

See how Ed Muzio explains the Bathtub Model himself in this video: https://bit.ly/2WEr9i0

In the next chapter, I will introduce three virtual pocket tools that you already have at your disposal. You just didn't realize that you had them.

Chapter 4.5: How to ease pains, repair damages and remove obstacles

Your primary concern as a leader is to attain the desired change and growth. Having all conditions in place from D.U.M.B. vision through S.M.A.R.T. action plan, what remains is to continually keep the stakeholders motivated in their collaboration to execute the action plan as agreed upon.

As a pragmatic leader, you keep meetings limited to a minimum in number and duration. I dare say you manage by exception (Bathtub Model, stakeholders know when and what to expect from you) and by walking around (actually and virtually).

Communication is the only way to manage the human factor. Depending on the environment, you choose the communication style that fits best, but you always remain the genuine you.

However, I do have three special virtual pocket tools for you. And I urge you to be overt about them. Just letting your stakeholders know you have them is enough, most of the time, to break any possible tension.

In one front pocket, you carry a jar of honey and in the other front pocket a tube of glue. And just to be sure, you carry a small penknife in your back pocket. All virtually, of course.

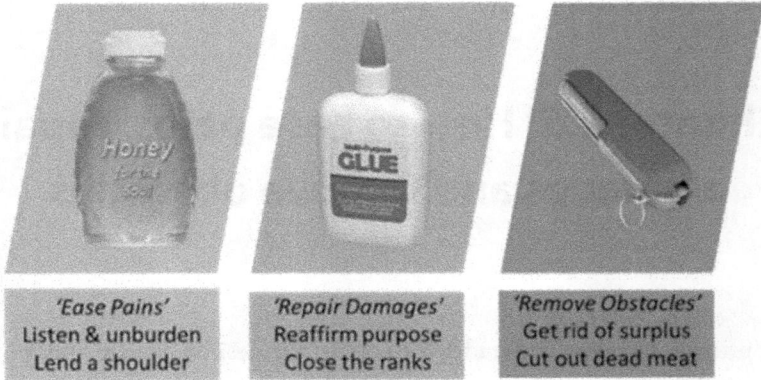

'Ease Pains'	'Repair Damages'	'Remove Obstacles'
Listen & unburden	Reaffirm purpose	Get rid of surplus
Lend a shoulder	Close the ranks	Cut out dead meat

Virtual Honey

Stakeholders are human beings just like you and me. They get frustrated at times due to their work or even their situation at home. Maybe they only need some attention and be heard. Maybe they need comforting.

You give attention, you listen to them, you comfort them, you lend them a shoulder, you unburden them, you reassure them, you compliment them. You ease their pains and give them a boost, and thereby secure their collaboration.

Virtual Glue

In their urge to excel or even in their fear to fail, sometimes stakeholders deviate from the plan. You have to get them back on track and reaffirm your purpose. Sometimes there are tensions between stakeholders. You must close the ranks. You must repair these kinds of damages in time to get the job done as agreed.

Virtual Penknife

This may not be your favorite tool and you rarely use it, but sometimes things get out of hand. Good is good enough regarding a healthy balance between time, cost, and quality. Expert team members tend to strive for often unnecessary or even unwanted excellence. Then you have to convince them to cut back or even instruct them to. Next, despite careful recruiting, it can happen that someone just doesn't fit on the team. Unfortunately, you have to dismiss this person. It's your responsibility to remove obstacles that stand in the way of achieving the goals agreed upon.

These virtual tools help you practice Pragmatic Leadership with a Wink. Here's where leadership is also having fun while playfully getting your point across. By actually telling your stakeholders that you use them, you break any tension, put a smile on their faces, and open the door to trust and accessibility. They know you are there for them.

I invite you to use these virtual pocket tools openly or define your own and see how it works for you.

Indeed no reference to anyone's video here. These virtual pocket tools are my own inventions. My experience is that every evening I virtually refill my jar of honey. I weekly get myself a new virtual tube of glue. And once a year I sharpen my virtual penknife.

At this point, you've made it through the main content of the Gear Pillar. What follows is some action taking, bonus material, and a case study. Just because I didn't denominate them as main content doesn't mean they are not important. They reinforce the main content. So take some time and go through them. The case study is a typical illustration of how a tailor-made assessment tool can secure the collaboration of reluctant stakeholders.

Your Gear Call-for-Action:
Optimize your toolbox, less is more!

➔ Use the right tool for the right job. ⬅

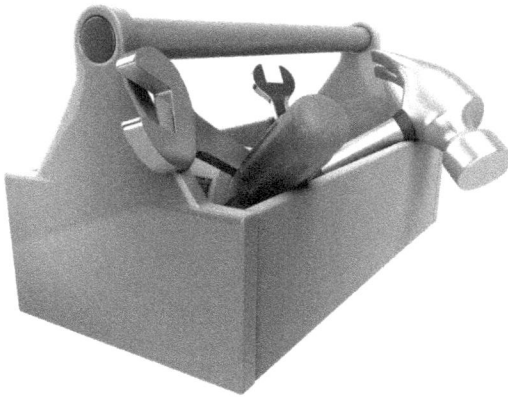

Your Gear Call-for-Reflection: Do your tools contribute to your bottom line?

Do you use your tools consistently?

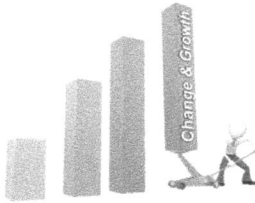

Do your stakeholders all use the same tools?

Do you evaluate the use of tools regularly?

Bonus Chapter 1: How to present the state of affairs

Often CEOs, higher management, sponsors and project leaders lack a simple instrument to show the status of their endeavors at one glance. There are many reporting tools out there, but most of them are rather complex and confusing to comprehend. And for a good reason. It's not an exact science because you are also dealing with humans. Trying to make it look like it's science makes it so complicated that nobody comprehends it. They get buried in facts and figures, what I call spreadsheet management. Therefore I've developed this simple and pragmatic status dashboard tool using KPIs and norms.

In my practice for decades leading major projects, I received the most understanding and the best compliments from my sponsors for reporting with such clarity and simplicity. Just one sheet of paper (or one screenshot) with a graphic and a short explanation!

The objective is to gain insight into the state of affairs at a glance using a simple high-level status report.

1. The Base

This approach only needs three agreed-upon components:

- Key Performance Indicators (KPI)
- Norm per KPI
- Reporting Schedule

First, you must establish the KPIs for the object you want to manage. Secondly, you must set the norm (value range) per KPI. And lastly, you must agree on the schedule (i.e. weekly, monthly) for the reporting of the results.

2. Examples of KPIs

- KPIs for projects: lead time, money (cost), quality, information, organization.
- KPIs for services: availability, response time, money (cost), quality.

3. Results

- Objective measurements per KPI relative to the norm.
- Status per management object (e.g. project, service), derived from the results per KPI.

4. Back-end Measurements Storage

Log the objective measurements of the KPIs in a spreadsheet. Be conservative in the number of KPIs you define. The less the better. Try to keep the number in the one-digit range. Keep it clear and simple or else it will slip away.

The same goes for the norm-setting. Be reasonable in the application of deviation ranges for the KPIs. Make the offered choices obvious to comprehend.

My experience is that it's quite easy to get agreement on the KPIs. The big discussions always concern the setting of the norms. Take enough time to get consensus on this. It will save you a lot of headaches later on.

These measurements and their assessment against the norms are the backings and the validation for the front-end display of the status results.

5.Front-end Results Dashboard

This is the fun part. Now we are going public. Make it easy to digest at a glance. Here's what I use and what anyone can understand regarding the meaning.

- Traffic lights per KPI Status
- Smileys for the Management Object Status

Yes, that simple! That's my state of affairs infographic I showcase where everyone can see it.

6. Attention Points

- There should be an obvious and visible consistency between "Traffic lights" and "Smileys". E.g., you can't have a red Smiley if all the Traffic lights are green! But you can have a red Smiley if at least one Traffic light is red. You catch my drift.
- At least every red result should be accompanied by a short explanation of why it is red and a suggestion how to get out of the red. Optionally, the same goes for the yellow/orange results.

BTW, if you get a legitimate red Smiley and you didn't see it coming, you were not doing your job well as a leader and now you take the heat!

7. Consideration

Selecting and choosing the right and meaningful KPIs for the object you want to manage is not only a question of logic, but also of experience and a bit of art. The latter is more about reading the environment and the stakeholders you have to deal with. Every situation is different, and stakeholders' interests vary. By nature, it's a subjective exercise.

Best practice is to reach a consensus with the significant stakeholders about the KPIs to be monitored and the norms to be applied per KPI.

You will have to practice the art of interpretation of the results to make meaningful decisions.

8. Recommendation

Showcase your Front-end Results Dashboard (Traffic lights and Smileys) openly where everyone can see it. That can be very motivating for your stakeholders and team, especially if Traffic lights and Smileys are predominantly green and no red.

On the other hand, showcasing can also work preventively. Nobody wants to be associated with red or even orange/yellow for that matter. They will do their best to avoid that once they know it will be showcased to everybody.

Bonus Chapter 2: How to evaluate a project to learn, not criticize

We have seen so many times that when a project is done everyone goes back to their daily duties. Nevertheless, any seasoned project leader will tell you that project evaluation is very useful at the end of the project. Still, many projects end without an evaluation or review. Why? Because most project leaders and project sponsors don't know how to do an evaluation and how they can benefit from that. In the case of a long-term project, I even believe you should plan a midterm evaluation.

1. Why Project Evaluation

A project evaluation's goal is to keep and secure the good and to learn from the mistakes. Following projects will benefit from that insight. Each project has a predefined goal and results to be achieved. Each project is carried out by a project staff and with a certain approach, in most cases described in a project plan.

A project evaluation will give insight into the outcomes of the project (the effect, to what extent the goals have been achieved), the performance of the project organization, and what project stakeholders, project staff or others can learn from the project.

A project evaluation can be performed in various ways. The two commonly used settings are:

- Using evaluation forms, which are individually completed by the project stakeholders and project staff. Optionally, the completed forms can be discussed in the project team.
- A more interactive setting for a project evaluation is to organize a brainstorming or brown paper session. In such a session the entire project team (or a representative delegation) will discuss the positive aspects of the project, and aspects which need to be improved. This setting will require the presence of a moderator to guide the discussion.

2. Components of Project Evaluation

- Looking back on the course of the process (time spent, jams, difficulties, windfalls, etc.).
- Assessing the quality of the final result (according to plan, sponsor and project team).
- Assessing how the different roles were carried out in the project.
- Assessing the level of increase in knowledge, and of gaps in knowledge and skills.
- Identifying the risks associated with possible improvements.
- Examining the project documentation and researching of gaps in the recorded information.
- Analyzing the statistical data related to time, money, quality, information and organization management.

3. Efficient Evaluation Approach

An efficient way to evaluate a project is to use evaluation forms and then discuss the completed forms in an interactive discussion. Having an evaluation form ready is one thing; organizing the interactive discussion session is another. Here I provide a generally usable project evaluation form that can be tailored to any specific situation.

Depending on the project environment, the representative stakeholders must be appointed to complete the evaluation form. Relevant stakeholders are sponsors, project staff, suppliers, and users of the project results.

4. Best Practice Procedure

- Let each stakeholder decide how they want to complete the evaluation form.
- Let each stakeholder appoint their representative to participate in the interactive discussion of the completed forms, together with the representatives of the other stakeholders.
- Appoint a moderator to guide the interactive discussion. Preferably an independent person.
- Set a timeframe for the interactive discussion. A two-hour period is a reasonable time to complete the discussion. This depends on the complexity of the project, of course.
- Let the moderator report the findings to all concerned.

Pay special attention to the money aspect of the project. Decide in advance whether this will be part of the evaluation. Often this is something specific between the sponsor and the project leader. Including the money aspect in the evaluation can distract from the other aspects.

5. Project Evaluation Form (PEF)

I offer my complimentary, generally usable project evaluation form as a proprietary MS Word document that can be tailored to fit any specific situation. In my model, I cover three project evaluation perspectives.

- Discrepancies regarding the four core content aspects of a project.
- Deviations in the five major management aspects of a project.
- Opinions on what went well and what could be improved by at least four types of project stakeholders.

Project Evaluation Form

A. Identified / Alleged Discrepancies regarding the project:	
1. Goal	
2. Scope	
3. Approach	
4. Results	

B. Deviations in the management aspects:	
1. Time	
2. Money	(Optional)
3. Quality	
4. Information	
5. Organization	

C. Opinions on what went well and what could be improved by *:	
1. Sponsor	
2. Project staff	
3. Users	

4. Suppliers	
5. Other relevant parties	(Optional)

* Examples of topics for an inventory of opinions:		
Project plan (good?) Planning (realistic?) People (right qualifications?)	Communication (enough & good?) Reporting (frequent & good?)	Consultation structure (correct and effective?) Unexpected problems/delays

Copy this form or use the link below to download as a MS Word document. https://bit.ly/2F3KX3M

Case Study: How a tailor-made assessment tool got me the collaboration of a reluctant team

The Client

A regional mental healthcare institution with resident and polyclinic patients. Staff is very dependent on IT and communication facilities to serve their patients effectively and efficiently. They support and maintain these facilities on their own and with an in-house IT and communication service department. They consider this a crucial factor in their successful operation.

The Challenge

The board decided that it's high time to modernize the complete IT and communication infrastructure to keep up with the competition and to be compliant with the new government rules on privacy.

The actual infrastructure is completely outdated, which means setting up a new infrastructure with the latest technology and equipment. That also means retraining the staff of the IT and communication service department and retraining the medical staff in how to use the new procedures and equipment. All to be fully operational within a year.

The board has been trying to implement these changes for the last couple of years, but the IT and communication staff held off the board by keeping operations running the old way without major issues. They kept on arguing that they can keep things going without new investments.

Nevertheless, the board finally persisted in following through with their plan. This time the board went looking for an external project manager to get the job done. In their selection procedure, they selected me due to my track record in IT and communication projects and my proposal on how to get the IT and communication staff on board.

My assignment was to get the IT and communication staff on board, select the most suitable infrastructure plus equipment, train the IT and communication staff to support and maintain the new technical environment, transfer all the operational and patient information to the new environment without disturbing daily operations, and instruct the medical staff in how to use the new environment. I had to report to the financial director, who was my formal project sponsor.

My Solution

I had enough experience with similar IT and communication projects. So I had no concerns about the technical and instructional aspects of the new infrastructure. That's all in a day's work, as they say. I could hire additional professionals to help out in the implementation phase. After all, I was chosen because of my experience and contacts in that field. The real technical challenge, so to speak, was selecting the most suitable infrastructure. The first thing I do in these cases is to hire an independent external IT and communication architect. I'm known for doing this. This architect serves as my right hand, my advisor, my technical conscience.

Nevertheless, the success of the whole mission was fully dependent on the cooperation and collaboration of the in-house IT and communication staff. Yes, they knew by now that there was no going back, but I still had to get them on board. To put it mildly, they were not amused by my presence.

I decided to kill two birds with one stone. I told the IT and communication staff that I wanted them—under the guidance of my architect—to decide which infrastructure would be suitable for the needs of the organization. After all, it would be their baby they'd have to nurture in the future.

I proposed that they define the requirements for the new infrastructure, they make a shortlist of potential contractors, and they define the assessment criteria and scoring method on how to choose the delivering contractor. In essence they should create a tailor-made assessment tool to select the most suitable infrastructure and delivery contractor.

I added that once we agree on all of that, we commit beforehand to the result that comes from that assessment, no matter what that result may be. I will preside over the hearings with the potential contractors, where the staff will also participate. I will also invite my project sponsor to attend. After the hearings I will present the scoring results in a joint meeting with the IT and communication staff and my project sponsor. The contractor with the highest score gets the contract to deliver and install the new infrastructure.

Then I told them to take my proposal and discuss it among themselves and let me know the next day if they agree to go along with it. Guess what? The next day early in the morning they came to me and told me they were on board. I shook their hands and told them that we now have a plan and a commitment, so let's get the ball rolling.

And that's the way we did it. For the purpose of this case study I will not go through all the details. But we selected a new infrastructure and the delivery contractor. Strikingly enough, it wasn't the choice they made off the cuff before the hearings. But they committed to the results of the scores.

The crux of this case is that I gave them my trust in their ability to take responsibility for making the right decision for themselves and their organization. They felt recognized and heard, that their opinion matters. And

I was sure they would take good care of their new infrastructure. Needless to say, I gained their trust too.

I now had a committed team that granted me the success of delivering a fully operational environment within the given timeframe.

The Results

The desired new infrastructure was delivered fully operational in the given timeframe within a year.

The board was happy with the outcome and can be assured that the IT and communication service department will take good care of their new infrastructure.

IT and communication staff are now more receptive to changes as long as they are involved in the process.

I got a farewell party with a buffet, a nice bottle of wine, and a book about the historical building in which the mental healthcare institution is located. I would say they were satisfied with my performance.

You, your stakeholders, environment, and tools are lined up! Ready at last?

Did you follow the pillars in the given order? Did you complete all your calls-for-action and calls-for-reflection? Then yes, you're finally all set to be successful in your endeavors and projects! Now you're a Performance Rocketeer!

For more encouragement, please take a few minutes to read the conclusion and follow-up chapter. And while you're at it, why not read out the book? The end of this book is just a few pages away.

The Pragmatic Leadership Formula™

PRAGMATIC LEADERSHIP FORMULA™

People-centered Approach To Leadership

$$Y+X=$$

PL = 3G + 5P + 2C

Take the Lead with a Wink

3G Mindset for Growth
Grit: it's all about people
Grip: read the environment
Gear: use the right tools
Know your WHY

5P Core Attitude
Positive: think challenge
Pro-active: think ahead
Passionate: from the heart
Pragmatic: good is enough
Planning: viable milestones
Blend in but be yourself

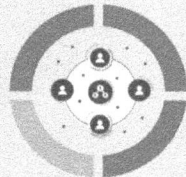

2C Secure Collaboration
Communication: connect always, everywhere, & listen
Commitment: secure & foster understanding of views/ideas
Together you can

Proven Leadership Formula to Skyrocket Team Performance and Boost your Net-worth, Self-worth, and Joy-worth

Conclusion and Follow-Up

Congratulations, you reached this far, so you finished reading the essential content of this book! I hope you took my advice on how to get the best experience with this interactive book. Now you have a competitive advantage on all your peers who haven't had the privilege of putting the insights you found in this book to work for them.

You learned how to get your mindset in success mode and make being successful a new habit. Driving your tribe to performance excellence is no longer a nightmare for you. Reading your operating environment to gain control is becoming second nature to you. And you now have some tools you can rely on to help you do all of that easier and faster.

I carefully crafted the proposed calls-for-action and calls-for-reflection to make sure you don't miss out on the main topics of the four pillars. If for some odd reason you didn't complete (some of) them, I urge you to go back and do so now. I promise you will benefit from it.

By following up with the action points, you now know what you have to work on to enhance your success in leading your tribe. I do not doubt that you also found other action points that fit your needs.

Maybe you read this book in one sitting to get an idea of what it's all about. You genuinely intend to come back later when you have more time for a more thorough study of the four pillars, and then take the appropriate action. And that's okay, as long as you come back and do your thing!

Listen, you and I know that tomorrow or next week never comes as we expect it to. Life has the habit of taking its course without any consideration. So do yourself a favor and block off the time on your calendar now while it's still at the top of your mind. Better be sure now than sorry later.

Imagine how you will stand six months from now, nine months from now, a year from now, with your next project. Still struggling as you did before? Or is your tribe finally excelling in performance due to your new approach?!

You know you found valuable nuggets to follow up on while reading, so please don't waste your investment in this book and let this opportunity slip away. You owe it to yourself, your business, your family, and your tribe to take action now.

Better yet, set a deadline for yourself in which you want to see the results of your follow-up actions. Then plan those actions on a timeline leading up to your deadline. Here's a tip to get you on your way. Write a Statement of Intent for this purpose as described in the Mindset Pillar, and visualize your intended success as your golden key!

The bottom line is, the improvement is not in the reading but the execution. Take action now and give it a shot. I can assure you that you will not regret it.

Need more help?

It's common knowledge that all successful people have multiple mentors and coaches to guide them and hold them accountable. No shame in that, but rather pride and gratitude.

I have mentors and coaches to keep me on track on different areas of expertise to help me grow my business. They are imperative to my success. I introduced three of them earlier in the overview chapter. In turn, I provide coaching and consulting to business and project managers when it comes to leadership and team performance.

In this book I provide you with valuable insights and information, so you have a good starting place to go it alone and make the best of it. Nevertheless, there are limits to what I can reasonably put in a book and to how far you can get on your own.

If you get stuck on the way, chances are you will give up. Every situation has its specific circumstances that require tailor-made approaches and solutions.

I'm here to tell you that you're not alone. Don't give up now that you know there is a way out. If you get stuck or you want to take the faster track, I'm here to help you. Getting my support may just be the catalyst you need to take you to the next level and beyond.

Check out the different options I offer at https://www.jawconsultancy.com and contact me from there. Together we will get on our way to new horizons with a tailor-made program to suit your particular needs.

About the Author

John A. Williams, MSc, aka "The Pragmaticioner" and best-selling author, is a seasoned project leader with decades of experience and more than a hundred successful and also a few failed major projects under his belt. He has gained the reputation of being a pragmatic leader and putting the human factor at the core of all his undertakings.

His signature Pragmatic Leadership Formula™, the foundation for this book, was quoted on mainstream news outlets. He has also developed a suite of proprietary self-assessment tools for leadership and supporting disciplines.

John was born and raised on the Caribbean island of Aruba, studied in Europe and found his base in The Netherlands. On his journeys to different parts of the world, he enriched himself with new cultures and insights. He now sees himself as a world citizen.

John's mission is to help others take the lead to success and satisfaction.

Acknowledgments

My humble thanks to the hundreds of team members I was privileged to lead and mentor over decades. They provided me with so much knowledge and wisdom in return.

A cordial thanks to the dozens of seasoned business and project managers who took their precious time to share their leadership experience with me.

I'd like to express my deep appreciation for the support and guidance from my prominent influencers Bob Proctor, John C. Maxwell, and Kevin Kruse for keeping me on track on matters of successful leadership. TR Garland and Susan Epstein for helping me focus on my message and mission. Lynda Goldman and Jay Magpantay for giving me the tools and guidance to get this book done.

My sincere gratitude goes to Douglas M. Brown, who was so readily willing to write the foreword for this book.

Invitation

THE
PRAGMA
TICIONER

For more valuable resources and tools to help you skyrocket your team performance, and in turn boost your net-worth, self-worth, and joy-worth, I invite you to visit my website https://www.jawconsultancy.com

A Kind Request

Thank you for reading this book. I hope you're on your way to skyrocket your team performance, and in turn boost your net-worth, self-worth, and joy-worth.

If you enjoyed this book, I'd be very grateful if you'd take a moment and post a short review. Here's a link to make it easier for you:

https://www.jawconsultancy.com/team-performance-review

Potential readers often depend on the experience of previous readers when deciding whether a book is for them. Your review will not only help them to make up their mind, but it will also help to set this book apart from other books in the same category.

It would mean a lot to me, and I very much appreciate you taking the time to write it!

From the heart,

John

Assessment Resources

Here are some proprietary self-assessment tools to help you evaluate and improve your skills and competencies regarding leadership, management and other supportive domains.

The assessments are set up as high-level self-evaluations to provide a flexible tool for monitoring and evaluating performance in a systematic and structured way. They are not harsh assessments but are self-evaluations from an empirical perspective (best practice). They can be used to identify areas of particularly good or poor practice and in establishing priorities for improvement action.

The assessment is done by evaluating the level of knowledge of or experience in the assessment elements and rating them on a scale of one to five. The first self-assessment can serve as a baseline for follow-up self-evaluations. The dated assessments can be a useful instrument to keep track of progress.

Below you will find a list of the assessment tools with a short description and grouped by the pillars they relate to.

To get any of these complimentary assessment tools, just visit https://www.jawconsultancy.com/assessment-tools

Assessments related to Pillar #1

STMA

Strategic Thinking Maturity Assessment (STMA) is a tool for assessing the maturity level of seven critical skills for strategic thinking, derived from the results of decades of research among strategic thinkers.

The seven critical skills for strategic thinking:

1. Logical & Creative
2. Vision & Purpose
3. Goals & Plans
4. Flexible Planner
5. Aware & Perceptive
6. Eager Learner
7. Coachable

LSA

The Leadership Skills Assessment (LSA) is a tool for assessing the ten leadership skills that distinguish great leaders.

The ten leadership skills that distinguish great leaders:

1. Vision
2. Passion
3. Confidence
4. Positivity
5. Persistence
6. Communication
7. Creativity
8. Independence
9. Integrity
10. Delegation

PMSA

The Project Management Skills Assessment (PMSA) is a tool for assessing ten behavioral and methodical skills of a successful project manager.

The ten behavioral and methodical skills of a successful project manager:

1. Analytical Thinking
2. Gathering Information
3. Planning & Organizing
4. Interdisciplinary Awareness
5. Communications
6. Project Management
7. Reporting
8. Risk Management
9. Scope & Quality
10. Planning & Control

PSMA

Project Sponsorship Maturity Assessment (PSMA) is a tool for assessing the maturity level of seven project sponsorship responsibilities, derived from the conclusions of a variety of international academic studies.

The seven project sponsorship responsibilities:

1. Purpose
2. Goals
3. Conditions
4. Engagement
5. Governance
6. Redemption
7. Communication

Assessments related to Pillar #2

LCAA

The Leadership Core Attitude Assessment (LCAA) is a tool for assessing the five core attitude characteristics of a pragmatic leader.

The five core attitude characteristics of a pragmatic leader:

1. Positive in Mindset
2. Pro-active in Action
3. Passionate in Purpose
4. Pragmatic in Execution
5. Planning in Delivery

CSA

The Communication Skills Assessment (CSA) is a tool for assessing communication skills based on the common five steps in the communication process.

The common five steps in the communication process:

1. Planning the Message
2. Crafting the Message
3. Delivering the Message
4. Interpreting the Message
5. Getting Feedback

TbMA

Team-building Maturity Assessment (TbMA) is a tool for assessing the maturity level of five team-building skills, derived from a set of fundamental beliefs, norms, rules and values that are accepted as true and that successful team-builders have in common.

The five team-building skills:

1. Understanding Team Dynamic
2. Recognizing Weak Links
3. Working with Other Groups
4. Communicating Effectively
5. Rewarding the Team

TMMA

Time Management Maturity Assessment (TMMA) is a tool for assessing the maturity level of seven basic action steps that high-level entrepreneurs take to manage their time profitably.

The seven time management basic action steps:

1. Setting Goals
2. Defining Tasks
3. Planning Actions
4. Eliminating Distractions
5. Automating Tasks
6. Delegating Tasks
7. Keeping Focus

Assessments related to Pillar #3

CMbSA

The Change Management Skills Assessment (CMbSA) is a tool for assessing four basic skills to manage change in an organization successfully.

The four basic skills to manage change:

1. Understanding change
2. Planning change
3. Managing resistance (to change)
4. Implementing change

CMMA

Change Management Maturity Assessment (CMMA) is a tool for assessing the maturity level of components of change in an organization, derived from the Knoster Model.

The Knoster Model distinguishes six components of change:

1. Vision
2. Consensus
3. Incentives
4. Skills
5. Resources
6. Action Plan

QMMA

Quality Management Maturity Assessment (QMMA) is a tool for assessing the maturity level of seven principles of Quality Management, derived from ISO's (International Standardization Organization) quality management standards.

The seven quality management principles:

1. Customer Focus
2. Leadership
3. People Engagement
4. Process Approach
5. Improvement
6. Evidence-Based Decision Making
7. Relationship Management

RMMA

Risk Management Maturity Assessment (RMMA) is a tool for assessing the maturity level of seven key maturity aspects of Risk Management, derived from the EFQM (European Foundation for Quality Management) Excellence Model.

The seven key risk management maturity aspects:

1. Leadership
2. Risk Strategy
3. People
4. Partnerships
5. Processes
6. Risk Handling
7. Outcomes

9 781988 645315